# TO TASTE, TO TOUCH, TO FEEL

Edited by

Rebecca Mee

First published in Great Britain in 2001 by
*POETRY NOW*
Remus House,
Coltsfoot Drive,
Peterborough, PE2 9JX
Telephone  (01733) 898101
Fax (01733) 313524

HB ISBN 0 75432 555 5
SB ISBN 0 75432 556 3

# FOREWORD

Although we are a nation of poets we are accused of not reading poetry, or buying poetry books. After many years of listening to the incessant gripes of poetry publishers, I can only assume that the books they publish, in general, are books that most people do not want to read.

Poetry should not be obscure, introverted, and as cryptic as a crossword puzzle: it is the poet's duty to reach out and embrace the world.

The world owes the poet nothing and we should not be expected to dig and delve into a rambling discourse searching for some inner meaning.

The reason we write poetry (and almost all of us do) is because we want to communicate: an ideal; an idea; or a specific feeling. Poetry is as essential in communication, as a letter; a radio; a telephone, and the main criterion for selecting the poems in this anthology is very simple: they communicate.

# CONTENTS

## THE GARDEN BEFORE RAIN

White crescendo.
The swan sedate
on dry land.

Daffodils throb heady yellow.

Muffled tread small twigs
among insignificant grasses,
heather-rattle,
stones muted grey, black
brick-brown.

The quaint polyphony of ducks
echoes like axe-blows
of distant quarry men.

Furious, the beat of wings.

A February chestnut leans aged arms
into dark green water,
lifts them
at an angry sky.

*Dal Strutt*

# TOUCH ME

Rain-fey breeze lifts
your hair
rustle yellow seed-grass
troubled times

a kiss, against all odds
race, we call our own
shadows hiding
at edge of ruined city

tugging call of river
your hand in mine
our first embrace
taken secretly

sky, slow and close
entwined in dark:
dust rising at dawn
pale pink in the sun

reflections in water
two faces rippling
stone sends rings
troubles spread away

light splintered away
two hands
slipping apart: back turned
we walk away

*T Webster*

## CREATION - LIFE

In swirling mists
born on winds
amidst the rumble
of hot and cold
electric friction of air
drawn by gravity's needs
falling
ever falling through the sky
to land on earth
giving forth life giving water

a raindrop in a thunderstorm

*Martin R Anderson*

## ROSELAND

This is an elemental place:
Beyond the path mist hangs on ragged oaks,
Sun burning white,
Turns vapours into daytime ghosts.
Here sea and cloud conjoin:
The tide, a muffled slap and shush,
Remains concealed.
There is a hush enveloping this scene -
As, in slack water herons wait,
A curlew's plaintive voice librates
Across an unseen sea.

Wind on a turning tide
Brings magic - smoke and mirrors -
Conjures up a fishing smack,
Chuntering through the beds of wrack,
For curtained mist to hide.
And from the distance
Tinkling song of sheet on mast,
St Anthony's low mournful moan;
As all the headland fog holds fast
Spirits and wraiths are free to roam.

*Patrick Osada*

# Soothing Surroundings

When the loudest thing
is a crow's flapping wing;
an endless spool of landscape
rolls across my vision.

When butterflies billow, forming soft frills,
with the rise and sweep of mist muffled hills;
every tiny sound of nature
echoes in my ear.

When bright poppies blaze in the morning sun
a blanket of lambs frolic in fun.
Sunbeams scatter diamonds
across the surface of the sea.

When bumble bees bask and drone
through summer air as still as stone;
a kaleidoscope of rainbows
play beneath my heavy lids.

When swallows skim, then glide unseen,
soft rain cries down on emerald green.
Soothed senses weave
and melt as one.

*Rosalind Smith*

## A Morning Cigar

The sun's a match
Under a magnifying glass,

The earth competes
With volcanoes,

But a morning cigar!

Heady and scented,
Lazy by choice of patience,

Teasing sleep
With alien dreams.

*Marylène Walker*

## AGAIN, THE GARDEN

Once more in the wild part of the garden
early on a summer's morning
I stand serene, enchanted
by more birdsong than I know.
Through the trees the climbing sun
paints swathes of life on brown and green,
picks out individual pearls of dew,
makes rainbows of the spiders' webs and
halos the bustling flies and bees with gold.
The place is simply beautiful.

Suddenly the war planes are there:
snaking across the heavens,
practising their low quicksilver manoeuvres.
They cast a fleeting, roaring, poisoning shadow
and are gone

leaving this man now rudely awakened.

*Stephen Eric Smyth*

## SMOKE ON THE MOON

Far misting copse now close appears
In crisp at even snowfall new and
Playing foxes, rusted, bark aloud . . .
Where high and proud and five a side
Stark fish-bone treetops wave, astride
A long and climbing avenue.

Three trooping brothers trundle in,
Pack and cape, to glad escape from
Blood and more, to damn the war
With all its din . . . bedraggled . . .
Reach the Coaching Inn . . .
As winter's chancing sun reclines,
To disembark in lantern-shine.

A coachman speaks of too much snow,
The horses can no further go.
Thus armed with pay and full of mirth,
There, troopers drink to peace on earth.
Their battles won, they rest awhile but
On then! . . . Over brook and stile . . .
As would all brothers, three abreast,
Across such, push and shove in jest!

Snow on snow, deep they go, away the styx!
With boot print six, cruel the blow in
Field on field now 'dot' they three . . .
The 'domino' . . . black on white in this night
Seeking out the city bright.
No cannon-fire in drift and spire but
Late, down rutted freezing shire, come . . .
Echoes of cathedral choir.

Now folding snows shift well aside
For bustling streets all cobbled wide,
Where 'easy-women' shout out loud and
Lamplit 'work' a bawdy crowd.
With breath of heated kettle-steam,
Thus, stand the three within a dream,
They search out, frosted lash and eye,
A tavern, with no tankard dry . . . and
Not 'too soon' do they espy
A sign which swings a pretty tune . . .
All writ in gold 'Smoke On The Moon'.

**Roger Mosedale**

## PLEASE SOMEONE LISTEN!

I sit in the shelter of an archway
With blanket and my dog at my side.
With my cigarette, cheese roll and my beer can
With nowhere safe and comfortable to abide.

Snow is falling around me
But this life is something befallen me.
There was no one there to assist me
No one listening to my plea.

Someone told me that someone does listen
But of this I have not found proof.
The world goes past me with disdain
Looking down on me and being aloof.

If there is someone listening to me
Why doesn't a reasonable answer come?
When Jesus was in the manger
Did he cry because he was numb?

I have pondered over such matters
And somehow my life never alters.
Sometimes I hear a voice
But the voice only makes me falter!

So I'll give my dog a bone
And settle down once again
Good heavens! The snow has gone!
And now it is pouring with rain!

*Beatrice Foot*

# IN COMFORT

A slight chill greets me
As I enter my room
My place in the world
Is this
In all its grandeur or in this singularly lacking
I have an electric fire
To this I turn
To warm the room
All mine with its chair
Its bed - not yet time
The cold outside
Comes in
This winter
From some choice of mine
My books and folders from which I would seek
Some possible advancement
Taken from their use
Neatly piled
As I would now seek to warm
A cup of tea
Fragrant and round it
Washes down my throat
The armchair big and comfortable, perhaps,
Delicious warmth now gathers me
I close the heavy curtains, clackety-clack
As a waft of warm delicious air reaches me
I am finally in comfort.

*C J Bayless*

## UNI-VERSE

The lustre of rare, sparkling gems,
Cut and polished, highly prized,
Can't compare with what I sense
When gazing deep into her eyes.

Cheering warmth of summer sun,
Verdant landscape, bolting hare,
Holding hands, we walk and run,
Cheeks aglow and free from care.

Butterflies just flutter by,
Bumbling bees collect their food;
Boeing trails across the sky,
Birds trill sweetly, where we're stood.

Strolling on, 'midst rolling dunes,
Soon to hear the ocean's roar,
Grasses whistle ancient tunes,
As footprints form, on sea-washed shore.

Dawdling, arm-in-arm, we tarry;
Lowering sun lays golden trail;
Wheeling seagulls thrust and parry;
Still, we watch, feet crunching shale.

Sky turns tangerine, deep blush,
Tinged with violet, indigo,
Frothing wavelets shoreward rush;
Back to sea they have to go!

Unstoppable, night's darkness looms,
Bejewelled by a myriad stars;
Our love fills universal rooms;
Let's have our summer house on Mars!

*Gareth Wynne Richards*

## AN IMPORTANT PART OF LIFE

The noise of cities, blaring music,
Flashing lights and roaring traffic,
Shouting slogans! Modern life's
Excitement crushes and swallows up,
Kills instinct and murders minds,
Destroys the urges to create,
Chains the body, blinds the eyes,
Deafens delicate hearing, poisons intestines,
A quiet forest, an empty beach,
An amazing field after field
Of endless space and beauty,
Its highest note will break glass mirrors,
Its powerful grandeur if you sit and look
And think and breathe and listen to
The sounds will help you hear this talking world.
And when you turn your mind to city life
To plastic noise and hype.
There is no comparison.
Who can compare a cloud
To man's poor, puny puff of smoke,
A plastic candle holder to a tree,
A lacquered eyelash to a rose,
A plastic bubble to a hill.
Until you view the mountains and the skies
And the thrill to the world through natural eyes
And know you are part of the picture
You will never be a very important part of life.

*Joan E Blissett*

# PETAL RAIN

Petal rain
Touched my senses
With her essence.
Petal rain
Tears of joy
The boy
I could have been.
Petal rain
Velvet mantle
Where I run, walk and rest.
Are you a paradise
Or a dream come true?
Tell me why
It's you.

**Paolo Debernardi**

## BLACK AND WHITE

If everything was black and white
How boring it would be!
No colours in the earth or sky,
No glory in the sea.

To look at things in monochrome,
No greens or browns or blues,
No sunset reds in heaven above
'Twould surely spoil our views.

But oh! Our Grand Creator knows
What's best for you and me.
So out of one man he made all
With great variety.

Red man, white man, yellow and black,
And all shades in between,
Without God's love and thoughtfulness . . .
We might have never been!

*E Balmain*

## CHANCIL PASS

By the cairn at the summit rests a youth
in the company of smiling shepherds.
Peaks fan out behind with plains to the south;
on the misty lake's margin graze goat herds.

Was I there? The celluloid is witness
but I can't remember the shutter's click.
Events before and after coalesce:
particles of furtive memory's trick.

Through deodar forests a rising trail,
trees thinning out into silver birches,
rainbow of meadow flowers in the vale,
again dark trunks as the steep way lurches.

Scent of wood smoke and the village appears:
harbinger of warmth, dissolver of years.

*Francis Pettitt*

## WINTER SOUNDS

Wet and windy winter with green and greasy ground;
Brown and broken bracken, and wheeling rooks around.
From high up on the Greensand, look south towards the Downs,
Over Rother Valley, now full of winter's sounds.

Far off noise of tractor that ploughs the Folkestone Bed;
Double boom of shotgun as clays from traps are sped.
Drone of busy traffic down on the Midhurst Road;
Growl of distant diesel that hauls a heavy load.

Static crackling pylons as ions are unloosed;
Flap of perching pigeon disturbed upon its roost.
Worried calls from cockerel who herds his hens to rest;
Angry buzz of chainsaw a long way to the west.

Tending shepherd talking to softly bleating sheep;
Raucous cry from pheasant startled from his sleep.
Quiet drip of droplets where silent silver rain
Gathers on the branches then falls to earth again.

Thus winter's sounds come seeping through dark and leafless trees
Painting winter's pictures more clearly than one sees.

*John Andre*

## COMPLETENESS

The wail of tears
Earth shattering
Yet tiny,
Helpless;
The wrinkled skin
Ugly
But enticingly beautiful
With eyes so big and wide
Begging to be loved;
The intoxicating aroma
Of clinical cleanliness
Newness and hope;
The soft hair beneath my lips
The finger tracing my mouth
Taste so innocent;
The skin, the hair,
The baby in my arms,
My son
Makes me feel . . .
. . . complete.

*Lindsey Brown*

## SHARING

Oh! What a truly wonderful thought
Of something that never can be bought,
The gift of one who wants to share
Knowing they do this with loving care,
To share our joy and ease our sorrow
Smooth the worries of tomorrow
Only God can really see
How this happened to you and me.

*J Boast*

# RAMELTON'S RIVERSIDE

Daylight shimmers through the trees
That shelter and envelop me.
Colours explode as the wind takes gust,
In greens, yellows, browns and rust.

Leaves kaleidoscope all around
And form a carpet on the ground.
Overhead the blackbirds soar,
Thunderous waves in the river roar.

Beyond the bridge a waterfall,
Mesmerises and enthrals,
Surging down into the deep,
Built in its side a Salmon Leap.

Patterns form as it crashes down,
Swirling, drowning round and round,
Freedom in its soul I see,
And visions of eternity.

***Gloria Donaghey***

## In Wintertime

In wintertime the trees stand bare,
dark limbs exposed to frosty air,
while dead leaves shrivel on the ground -
the better to be kicked around
by little boys with time to spare.

The fox lies trembling in his lair,
his ears pricked up, his nose aware
of scent and sound - of horse and hound
in wintertime.

But sad earth dormant everywhere,
worn down by months of wear and tear,
cares not - tho' leafless woods resound
to grunts from huntsmen, hooves that pound,
and children's laughter here and there
in wintertime.

*Sheila Burnett*

## ORB, REBORROWED

Before we forget the surrounding world
A memory on what forgot in man-structured
View and lost horizons
In the fractured reaches much shaped by the lost and tortured

Beauties reformed in scientific horrors
Cannot from the past borrow
And genetic reconstruction cannot reveal
The joys inborn that did not pass or

Dream from the past
Were renewed as our inheritance
Made more real in touch and sound
And even so with a smile or glance

The soft winds unseen in flower or leaf
The torrents rushing in steep power
The new sunrise uplifting in surprise
The short hour of brilliance scented flower

And more reflected past-sailing cloud
A starry scene obscuring more sharp light
The mystery even welcomed in dark rays
That mark our days

And when these messages of a life
Beyond us touch our feeble senses
Tell now in vacant reminiscences, in human sentence
In brief sentences.

*John Amsden*

# A HOUSEWIFE'S FAVOURITE THINGS!

A garden free of weeds after a day on my knees,
Pegged, crisp, white pillowcases billowing in the breeze.
A white feathery jet-stream etched in an azure sky,
Sunny fried eggs sizzling side by side.
Hot crumpets oozing butter from pincushion holes,
The sight of all these bring pleasure to my soul!

A sniff of cold chicken as I open the fridge door,
The smell of lavender beeswax on my newly-polished floor.
The freshness of washing as I unload the machine,
The scent of indoor flowers with green fern between.
The wafting aroma of a beef stew with dumplings,
All these gorgeous smells set my nostrils pumping!

The firmness of cooking apples picked from our tree,
The small round rear of my grandson on my knee,
The snugness of the electric blanket as I slide into bed,
The warm, soothing stream from the shower on my head.
The tight grip of a baby's hand around my finger,
All these sensations I wish would linger!

The tongue-tingle of fresh loganberries picked for tea,
Succulent roast lamb in a lake of minted peas.
Hot scones from the oven with cream and strawberry jam,
A great dollop of mustard on my wafer-thin ham.
Hot chocolate in a mug as I settle for the night,
All these delicacies serve my taste-buds right!

My grandson singing new songs learnt at school,
My son's hearty laughter watching a TV fool.
The plop of the morning post through the letter box,
The welcome turn of my husband's key in the lock.
The delightful silence that meets the end of the day,
These are the sounds I love coming my way!

*Pat Heppel*

## CREATION

I see in reflection His glory
when the sun lends the ocean its flame
and the spray breaks in fragments of colour
as it rises to honour His name

He speaks in the call of the curlew
in the whisper of wave upon sand
in the silence that follows the thunder
in the breeze that caresses the land

His touch comes through those that we care for
in the brush of a hand on your cheek
through the closeness and trust of another,
we dimly find Him whom we seek

By His life, he gives life to creation
yet in Him, all creation is held;
when the time we have here is completed,
then He will become our whole world.

In His eyes we will see dappled sunlight
in His voice hear the wind on the sea
in His presence we'll find only freedom
to become what He wants us to be

In His touch is the breeze on the cornfield
in His fragrance are summers long past;
in His love we can meet with each other
in His arms we find comfort at last

In this world, He is in all creation
yet our vision of Him remains dim:
He is alpha, omega, eternal
and continually draws us to Him.

*Alix Brown*

# A GIFT OF THE SENSES

To feel a clear and sparkling spring,
Trickle through my toes.
Lavender and honeysuckle,
The scent, pervades my nose.

To see the sun arising,
In the Eastern sky.
To hear a cuckoo calling,
Or a new born baby cry.

Taste buds working over time,
For home-made crusty bread.
The luxury of laundered sheets,
I feel upon my bed.

We must never take for granted,
The senses we are given.
To think and feel, to see and hear,
These gifts are made in heaven.

*Peggy Howe*

## QUIET CORNER

There's a corner of my garden
A cosy little nook,
Where I often take my ease
To knit or read a book.

I've contemplated patterns,
On that seat beneath the tree,
A blackbird's song, a clear blue sky
Or what to have for tea.

I iron out knotty problems
Solve crosswords by the score,
Darn old socks, check recipes
Chat to the girl next door.

World affairs are quite forgotten
And time scurries on a pace,
When I'm lost in contemplation
In my little thinking place.

*D A Sheasby*

## THIS PAGE OF SUMMER

This page of summer stands
Ringed round with gold: it is
Recorded by families of birds
And the leaves greater families.

It is spoken by every sail of cloud
Charting the endless sky;
Even the lizard, waking, blinks
A marvelling green eye.

Though the rest of the summer goes down
In a thousand miles of song,
This is the day my heart will remember
All winter long.

*Pamela Constantine*

# Snow 2000

A rare opportunity of a cold winter
Lots of snow in 2000 a freeze
Not like the usual wet and mild season
Which we are used to in days like these

Carbon dioxide and such in the air
Makes snow a rare treat this time of year
Enjoying it all as best I can
For next time may be in 2010

Washing freezing on the line
Feeling the ice beneath my shoes
But New Year's Eve brings wet windy weather
Of the kind we're used to, those mild weather blues.

*H G Griffiths*

## LET THE SPIDER SPIN!

What a waste of my time, this spring cleaning,
there is much more light in this life than gloom.
Birds know it, weaving nests with nature's loom.
I would rather spend my time redeeming
my garden, from winter's frozen dreaming
than wield mop and bucket, duster and broom
around the clutter of each cosy room;
keeping a spring day forever gleaming
with something more exciting to enjoy,
besides kowtow to a snob's opinion!
I don't expect special effort from them!
I do not decry the time they employ
In destroying the spider's dominion!
Let their intricate webs adorn my den.

*Valerie McKinley*

## TAILING ME

They climb into a boat
In their hot pursuance
To tail me
Here they come - the whales' nuisance

Seeking me out way here
They don't ever give up
The whalers
Succeed in a kill - they take their sup

Armed with their long sharp spears
All to throw and stab me
They try on
Separating me from family

I charge their boat in anger
But a stab stops me in my path
Why do they
Disturb my morning bath

I'm more than four times their weight
I think they're very brave
I could so
Tip their boat and not become their slave

Why not try to see it
From we whales' point of view
We did not
Set out to pursue and tail you.

They have no caring - sadly
To their greedy menu
They want to add me.

*Barbara Sherlow*

## THE ENCHANTMENT OF THE STARS

Beyond all reproduction by even the greatest artists
as viewed now by me from deepest countryside
is the moonless, cloudless starry sky.
Millions of celestial diamonds glitter as the jewellery
of the universe, invoking in me a joyous humility
as I envisage infinite space and time.

I feel no longings such as in summer sunshine,
that enticement to strip to nakedness of body
and loll in skin deep lasciviousness.

Nor am I pulsated with garden moonlight
to relive reminiscences of skin-soft romance
under the full orb's pallor.

Now, it is the nakedness of my exposed soul
that bathes, mystically, in an ethereal radiance
of heavenly rays of infinity,
pouring down life's eternal purpose, reality
beyond all human comprehension, the eternal
love of the creative God.

*Andrew Kerr*

# THE WORLD AS WE KNOW IT

Our world is the beauty of the earth's domain
It's green and lush, the breathtaking sight of a lifetime.
We take this beauty and crush it like we all went insane
No one's to blame for there's no reason or rhyme

We build and bomb and leave our land in the hands of devastation
We hear no cries for help or feel those people's pain
After carnage and retribution, we have our recreation
Some people try to tell, but their words are all in vain.

If only things were different, if only we could see
The beauty and the culture given to you and me.
It just takes a little study, a few people holding hands
To really get together and save our precious land.

For it truly is a wonder and it's given to us for free
So let rich and poor contribute to start our lives anew.
Let's look around in wonder and save each special tree
For we all have the power, yes even you and me.

*E Corr*

## THE WEE VILLAGE OF ABINGTON

There's a wee village in Lanarkshire
That has a small stream
It is an idyllic village that looks it's in a dream
The people are wonderful, it has so many charms
Pretty gardens, rambling plants and a welcome with open arms
The small post office sells a range of things
The hotel doubles up as a pub
Where the locals meet, drink and sing
Abington is a Scottish village of paradise
There you can stay in peace
A wonder in a green land
Where harmony will never cease.

*Pauline Edwards*

## WINTER SUN

Sunlight on the wallpaper,
the plant's delicate grey shadow
on the wallpaper,
the shadow of the pot,
the bright mortal green of the plant,
the unearthly beauty of the Handel duet,
the glint of the sun on the broadest green leaf,
the black and white pattern on the pot,
the reconciliation in this vision,
the sun pouring in
from the vast wintry sky
through the window in its frame,
the sunlight on the wallpaper,
the wallpaper a fixed world in relief,
the delicate grey shadow of the plant,
the delicate mortal green of the broad-leaved plant
in its black and white pot of reconciliation,
the mortality of the person watching,
the vast wintry sunlit sky,
the photographic sunlight
fixing the vision
of the ordinary world
in the wondering mind
for all time,
the absence of time

*Neville Davis*

# FOR GIVE - FOR GET - FOR GRACE

Forgive you?
Why should I?
How could I?
Have you repented?
Will you hurt me again?

Who suffers more?
The one who asks for forgiveness
But being rejected and ignored
Or the one who keeps the bitter memory
And the heavy scar in the heart?

Help me
How can I forget this nightmare?
Unless you forgive
You can't forget
And leave the haunting shadow

How can I forgive
without your repentance?
Remember Her
For She, the Lord our God died for us all
On the cross
On the cross
She suffered and forgave
Why not we?

*Mei Yuk Wong*

## RETIREMENT

The wheels of life run swiftly
In living our heyday,
But when we only chug along
'Tis said we've 'had our day'.

What we lack in agility
Experience we have gained
To broaden out our interest
Sensitivity is trained.

The sunshine and the showers,
The rainbow's fleeting show,
The dark of night-time hours,
The gleaming white of snow.

And in this great rotating world
Live creatures by the score
And each species is different
Life cannot be a bore!

*L Robinson*

# A WALK WITH NATURE

Sheltered from the stormy blast
Of modern bustling ways,
The rambler finds tranquillity
Within his every gaze.

Leafy trees stand tall and slender
By the trickling stream,
The nodding ferns sway to and fro
And beckon him to dream.

The waxy water lilies shine
Within the sun's warm glow,
The graceful swan protects her young
Where reeds and rushes grow.

A dark cloud settles overhead,
But cannot mar the view,
The walker knows within his heart,
That this is nature too!

The thunder cracks! The heavens pour,
The clouds then slowly drift away,
The storm subsides and in the silence;
Dawns another perfect day.

*Marian Theodora Maddison*

## OUR FIVE SENSES

I love the feel of silky soft fur
between my fingers when stroking the cat,
I love the creamy taste of a mouthful
of strawberry dessert,
I love the sight of a golden sunset:
it's like the brush strokes of a beautiful painting
spread across the sky.
I love the heavenly sound of a choir
singing in perfect harmony,
What can compare with the sweet fragrance
of roses on a summer's evening?

Touch, taste, sight, sound, smell -
we're so blessed if we have all five of them.
May we never cease to appreciate
the simple pleasures of life:
they are the backbone of our existence,
the bread and butter of what it means to be alive!

*Cathy Mearman*

## SUMMER LONGING

Oh to be up on a hillside green
On a glorious summer day!
With not a single main road to be seen
And the work-place far away
And silence all round, calm and serene,
Save the farmer cutting hay

And the song of the birds; and the lovely view
Would consist of fields, and they
Would have in them wheat and animals too.
Trees would line the winding way
Of the river's banks, and the houses few
Would be picked out in gold and grey.

Beautiful flowers I would see,
More beautiful than in May,
Wonderful scents would be all round me,
More lovely than I can say.
Oh, this is where I would like to be
On a glorious summer day!

*Jillian Mounter*

## SWEET RED ROSE

Red roses
Single or in a bunch
Vermilion perfumes
Fragrances of love
Sanguine petals like drops of blood
Bonded together in the essence of beauty

Protective thorns
Hiding age-old secrets
So divine and upright
In any position it stands apart
Shining sweet red rose
Never to be removed from its rightful place
With an outstanding, attractive scent
Amongst so many varied colourful flowers

Embedded in its delicate little core
Elegance and style
A truthful flower of romance
'Tis a sincere gift
When you've fallen truly
Then gracefully presenting
This unique red rose
Comes with a heavenly blessing from above
When our hearts have fallen madly in love . . .

*Frank G Romano*

## CADER IDRIS

She stands in splendour, gaunt against the sky
And contemplates the shallow lives of men
Her rocky skirts reach down to greet the cwm
Where shepherds wander tending flocks of sheep
Daily passing without a single glance
She carefully guards a hidden treasure
A sparkling lake, like the Creator's eye
Wet, for the sorrows of His lovely world.

*Wendy Dedicott*

## BLIND GARDEN

I am blind,
But in the garden of the mind,
I still can see sunflowers
And taste the April showers,
Touch the roughness of the flowers,
Feel the rose's prickly thorn
And on my inability to see pour scorn,
Am I one of the only few,
Who's never seen the morning dew?
I can't distinguish April from May,
But inside my head,
My imagination is not dead,
Colours blossom in my mind,
Colours no one can ever find,
Fragrances bring on powerful illusion,
To aid me in my delusion,
To me there is no confusion,
Segmenting together daisy chain,
Oh how clever is my brain,
When winter freezes solid ground,
A daffodil blooms all year round
And oh how graceful is the sound,
Of the busy bee,
I do not need eyes that I may see.

*Alan Pow*

## LITTLE

If I were a little tributary
finding my way into the great river
who was desperate
to swim into the strength of the seas
so I could flow
around the magnificent oceans
of this world
and the next,
forever,
together, I would be
as one with you.

*Annette M Wilson-Ford*

# A NEW DAY

In the morning my eyes open to a new day,
Outside a smell of fresh air,
Passing through my lungs making me feel fine,
My ears stand up as the robin sings.
Touching clean white snow upon the lawn,
Sends a chill right up my spine.
Time to go inside for breakfast and a cup of tea.
A welcome indeed.

*G F Snook*

## MY WORLD

There are no colours.
The day, the night
Are grey and black.
My world, my sightless world.

I live my life
Through touch, through taste,
By smell and sound.
My world, my sightless world.

The spring brings warm rain,
Summer, skin searing heat.
Autumn is damp, musty leaves,
Winter, iced fingers on my cheek.

The flowers in the room are fresh.
I know that he is here before he speaks.
I take from him the posy that he holds.
He tells me they are freesias, red and gold.

I trace my fingers round his oval face.
He tilts my chin and offers me a kiss,
Sings praises to the beauty that is me,
The mirror image I will never see.

There are no colours.
The day, the night
Are grey and black.
My world, my sightless world.

I live my life
Through touch, through taste,
By smell and sound,
But I am loved
And know that I am safe
In my world, my sightless world.

*Joyce Walker*

## HERE'S TO OUR WORLD

Here's to our world
The beauty of all beauties.
An island in space
The home of all our countries.
May her people's love surround her
With dignity and grace.
Everyone is proud of her
As she spins along in space.

Here's to our world
So precious and so lovely.
All through the years;
The sun, her royal trophy.
May her reign be long and wonderful
As she journeys on her way;
Her destiny the universe
As she rides the milky way.

And with her moon beside her
She fills our hearts with pride.
Raise your glasses and salute her
For she's our life - our world!

*Nelson*

## TO A ROSE

World, it is filled,
an expanding confusion
of things, things.

But you,
rose in my hand,
crystal tear in my heart,
are not of these.

*Louise Rogers*

## ON MY CANVAS

On my canvas is appearing
        A delightful rural view.
I would find it very cheering,
        If the picture could be true:
A landscape of great beauty,
        In the sunlight, features gleam,
Unspoiled, idyllic scenery,
        Passing through, a gentle stream.
This is glorious perfection
        And is matched by humankind,
Each one taking new direction,
        Having perfect peace in mind.
In one corner, there's a lame man,
        Grateful for a helping hand,
On the other side, for his gran,
        Is a young one on errand.
All will give consideration
        To their neighbours in their need
And seeking co-operation
        As each does in life proceed.
But, in this world of ours today,
        Can there be such unity?
Were man to really find God's way,
        There'd be glorious harmony.

*D J Price*

## DAWN CHORUS

In the quietness of the morning
When folk are still asleep
I stroll into the garden
Where the air is fresh and sweet
And there within the stillness
I listen to every sound
Birds have left their little nests
And are fluttering around
Perched high upon the treetops
They trill with notes so clear
And I stand in awe and wonder
At the marvellous sounds I hear.
The chorus of God's creatures
Fills my heart with glee
And I treasure every moment
When there's just the birds and me.

*Pat Harlow*

## BLACKCAP

On these broad hills, warm and rounded,
      That forever seem to say,
'I shall never be confounded,'
      I take my flower-strewn way.

And on one side there's the ocean,
      And on one a shining plain,
With a shadow-shifting motion,
      Like a thought beyond the brain.

And it seems to run forever
      To a place the heart might be,
While the sturdy hills still sever
      Its dominion from the sea.

And I feel its dappled music
      In the stirrings of my soul,
And a legend, dark and tragic,
      That will lead me to my goal.

Far above, the drove road harrows
      The whale-backed downland crest,
With its tumuli and barrows,
      On its journey to the west.

And I feel the lure of ages
      Where the ancients used to go,
And the idle heart engages
      With their archetypal flow.

For eternity surrounds them
      Where their timeless glory lies,
And there's nothing to confound them
      If their legend never dies.

*S H Smith*

## FROM WINTER INTO SPRING

There was a keen frost last evening
Yet the sun shines bright today.
It is the month of January
Almost one month since shortest day.

There is a hint of early spring;
The days begin to lengthen,
Winter pansies and primroses at their best,
A tree in the park just breaking into blossom.

The beauty of the landscape now is so inviting,
I see the lake and feel that spring is in the air.
Tonight's first lunar eclipse of the 21st century
Promises to be a spectacular event.

As earth crosses between sun and moon,
We see again the wonders of creation.
Tomorrow we will see the world again,
In all her fairness and beauty.

While in the press we have the holiday advertisements,
Beckoning us to lands afar;
Or to the beauty of the English countryside,
Complete to face the world again.

*Janet Cavill*

# THE ROCKING CHAIR

Rocking gently,
In the blazing summer sunshine,
Lounging without reverance
In the sumptuous padding
Of the worn wicker rocking chair.
Gazing through the blushing clematis,
Arching my own little Eden.
My head is filled,
With a sensory delight,
There is a barrage of sweet aromas,
Tantalising my perceptions.
A door creaks,
A radio hums in the distance,
A father yells -
A child cries.
A dog barks,
Yet all fill me with contented peace.
The birds serenade me sweetly.
Rocking in the old rocking chair,
Life unleashes its own brand of magic.

*Claire Partridge*

# BORDERS' BEAUTY TO BOOT

Walking in the Scottish Borders
Is a delight to all who stop and stare
The red of the robin, in hedgerows abound
Its beauty steals all around
The crisp sound of Boot on snow
'Tis Christmas time, as bells ring out
Crunch, crunch the Boot does shout
To cover another mile of wondrous scene
Of trees, as gaunt and bare, a screen
Against the biting wind, a sound of God,
White hills of glistening, crystal snow
As Boot steps out, still a long way to go.

Still further, through the whitening lane
Does the faithful Boot warmly gain
The smell of a sweating horse
The muffled clip, clop of hooves
On frozen tufted grass
A cheery 'Happy Christmas' from rider above
But still the Boot goes on and on
Blue sky high, of sun and love
Of the countryside - tranquil - still
The boot again stops and stares
Walking in the Scottish Borders
A heavenly way to heed God's orders.

*Dennis R Rowe*

## THE WORLD WE LIVE IN

Such wonderful sensations uplift us
When we think of our, wonderful world
Treasures of this and that are buried beneath us
In plentiful array to behold

Nature becomes a credit to the living world
One can visualise a great quantity
Mesmerising scene of our beautiful world
It has features of captivating quality

Law abiding scenes are frequent
But, the world takes it all in its stride
Rowdy people are at night frequent
Yet, the world can take them for a ride

The world is very ancient and well worn
Lots of its precious materials
Have been manufactured and well worn
But, it still carries on and endures its trials

Mother Earth plays havoc with our sinful ways
Sending earthquakes, hurricanes, blizzards and floods
Knocking the stuffing out of our hearts in many ways
We have to endure them, not put our heads in
          forgetting hoods

At all times the world makes life tricky
Being active and full of life misdemeanours
Twisting the good with the bad life's tricks
It has the better of us in the end, it is life's
          best cleaners

So the world we live in
Is full of great renown
Gives and takes away blessings
Some, put in the bin, others in the
        Guinness book, written down!

*Alma Montgomery Frank*

## FROST

Ice-crusted windows,
So I cannot see white frost
On backs of cattle
Crowding by the crew-yard doors
Until I go to feed them.

Green grass now turned white
After overnight hard frost
Lies flat in bright sun
And water carried for calves
Squelches icy in my boots.

On pond's smooth surface
A thick lid of ice has formed
Which winter's weak sun
Fails to melt . . . and skidding ducks
Make futile swimming motions.

*Dan Pugh*

## COWBOY HORIZON

I dream of Wild West movies
Recreated in the Arizona landscape.
Roaring red rocks recalling
Outlaw days of treachery,
Scorching heat, infamous legends and
Good versus evil. White hat always triumphs.
The vastness of the place overwhelms
My body, mind and soul.
I am dwarfed by these stupendous dimensions
Created by the natural world.
Terracotta terrain blasting my vision.
My voice echo-booms all around me.
Sweat pours down my back like summer showers.
My mind loses track of the hours
As I am lost in a timeless place.
My mouth is dry, dusty.
I can taste the rusty-coloured rocks
Upon my tongue. Their influence has
Seeped within my pores.
The doors of my mind have been opened
To seek enlightenment. But I need not
Look any further. I have found it within
This wondrous place.
Saguaro cactus stand tall and menacing
With their vicious succulence.
Sedona desert saturates
My senses. I am never the same again.

*Debbie Perks*

# WOODLAND PATH

A delightful sylvan entrance
Of beech trees tall and proud,
Gives a welcome to the path
Greeted by heads all bowed,
Scented bluebells everywhere
Swaying gently in the breeze,
Anemones join in the throng
Beneath the lovely trees,
Soft green leaves reaching out
Warming in the soft sunlight,
Branches entwine their spindly arms
Allowing little light,
To slip through the canopy
Transforming woodland scene,
Darkening the ground below
Where snowdrops once have been,
The woodland has so much to give
To creatures large and small,
Extraordinary flora
That grows both small and tall.

*J Naylor*

## A PICTURESQUE WALK

Crackling, rustling leaves, frozen frosted grass beneath my feet,
As I entered friendly local woods the other morning.
Sun was swiftly shimmering through the trees onto the ground,
Exhaled, I could taste coldness as it swept through my body.
Reached out to stroke tree bark, recoiled in horror at its wet feel,
Nose began to run as I smelt the freshness of the day.
A walk in the woods - an encompassing experience.

*S Mullinger*

## THE RED ROSE

The solitary rose glistened,
Red petals brimming with moisture,
Its sweet aroma sifting like sunshine
Across the crowded room.
Long gone spirits lingered with the fragrance,
As the dance commenced.
Lovers now swept together,
Dancing, as the music and fragrance entwined their souls.
This solitary rose,
Gleaned together all the sweetness
Of every dancing soul.
Storing deep inside the velvety bloom,
Untold mysteries of the paradise of love.

*Patricia Gargan Spencer*

## AUTUMN

The earth is covered with gold and brown leaves
that crunch like cornflakes at each footfall.
Mossy trunks rise from the barren earth
each vein starkly illuminated by shafts of golden sunshine
slanting through the trees.

Clumps of tenacious leaves on almost bare branches
are deep patches of colour etched against a clear bright blue sky.
The unmistakable odour of nature in decline assails the nostrils
and the breeze has a bite that leaves a cool film across the cheek.
It's autumn.

*Lesley Gill*

## AROMAS IN THE AIR

Aromas drift in sweet abandon gently floating in the air
Creating flights of fancy each and every one can share
Fragrant perfumes in a garden at the closing of the day
A walk of simple pleasure through a field of new mown hay.

A morning stroll through orchard ripe with fruit and berries plump
Rich odours of a grassy field around the water pump
What a joy to slowly wander through a peaceful bluebell wood
Its delicate aroma filled the air just where I stood.

Wild blossoms in the hedgerows on a quiet country lane
The sweetly scented roses around a windowpane
Droplets of a warming shower, diamond glints upon the leaves
Smell of woody perfume on the hedges and the trees.

An aroma fresh and pure at the ending of a storm
Baking cakes and crusty bread in a kitchen bright and warm
The wafting smells of barbecue - oh what a lovely treat
Mouth-watering smells of onions and of juicy dribbling meat.

An evening romp through meadow lush with my faithful old pal Rover
To know the musky smell of moss, the sweet smell of the clover
Whiffs of trickling petrol when 'filling up the car'
The surface of a new laid road, the heady smell of tar.

Smells that float upon the air are there for all to savour
Each one so very different from the odour of its neighbour
But each one giving pleasure with the perfumes they expel
Thank you God - we thank you, for the blessed sense of smell.

*Barbara Davies*

## OUR SURROUNDING WORLD

To wander through the bluebell woods
And walk the country lanes
Gives me a sense of freedom
That I cannot explain

To see the rolling fields
Or sit near a flowing stream
Creates tranquillity and peace for me
I wouldn't want to live in town
With busy shops and bustling crowds
Where life's so fast no time to stop
The noise from traffic so loud

Yet so much of our countryside
Is being built upon
It's so sad for our wildlife
Who will have nowhere to run
They are building on the land
That once they thought was home

*Gillian Morrisey*

## THE OAK TREE

From a tiny acorn you grew,
So many years ago.
Taller than a house you now stand,
The rings within your trunk
Will tell your age.

Your gnarled trunk,
Your mighty boughs,
Stretch out to feel the rain,
That when the sun appears,
Glisten like diamonds upon your leaves.

In autumn your leaves of soft green,
Turn to autumn shades,
Of red, brown and yellow.
Squirrels nest way up high,
Swinging from bough to bough,
Hiding acorns in the ground.

Around your feet some will grow
Into tiny oaks.
Another mighty oak to start its life.
Toadstools too grow around your roots,
The mice to nibble and take their fill.

Then man, will one day come
And you'll be chopped down.
Your trunk, a table make,
Some chairs, maybe a bed,
So many things,
That man can make from your mighty trunk.

Best of all,
I like you best,
When in a wood you stand,
With birds and squirrels in your boughs
And snow a mantle round your feet.

*J O Peart*

# TO THE RHYTHM OF LIFE

Far from the land I love, where the sun shines
every day
The people, young and old, smile to the rhythm
of life,
Dance to the happiness of their souls,
Move to the temperament of the sun,
Make love to the happiness of their hearts,
Kiss with meaning, talk with rhymes.
Slow with time, forget their worries quickly,
live longer.
Happiness is their goal.

*A F Goolsby*

## LIGHT IN OUR LIFE

In our inner mind comes many grand things to abound
A feeling of absolute beauty of sight and sound
To watch a sunrise in the morning and the setting at night
Warmth, beauty and light of the wonders of sight

Without sight we should lose so much of life
When we wake, new things to see, to feel so right
Even a small thing can have untold beauty for each one
While magnificent mountains and hills shine under the sun

Birds singing their hearts out, preening and cleaning away
Children shouting and singing outside in play
Then trooping off to school in uniform together
The start of new brain awakening whatever the weather

Looking at new things arriving in the store
Clothes, food, furniture and lots, lots more
To see, feel and pick out our favourite choice
Speaking in thanks in a thankful voice

In some food shops to pick fruit, cheese, new things to taste
Appreciating it all while there is no waste
Having all our senses on the alert while time does pass
Sitting outside on a strip of green grass.

*Bessie Groves*

## GOD GAVE ME EYES

God gave me eyes,
To see, to help others
To help, to care for
My sisters and brothers
God gave me eyes,
To see all beauty
To create, to write
Through his eyes we see
I close my eyes, when
I experience pain
God gave me tears of
Joy, hurt and strain
God gave me, light
Even in darkness
God gave me a second sight,
Made me see more
Made me see what I'm here for
God gave me eyes to see
To help someone on
God gave me eyes
A vision and a reason

*D Riches*

## THE SENSES

How wonderful to touch and feel
The softness of silk or a slippery eel,
Fingers gliding over fresh cut grass
All gone, so soon, alas, alas!

Then to sample some new made bread
The lovely taste invades your head,
Then add to this, some fresh butter
It sends your taste buds all aflutter.

A beautiful flower garden, such a special sight
All swaying and dancing in the golden light
Look upon this with awe and wonder
All around you and over yonder.

So many sounds are all around us
Our ears attentive to the fuss,
Cooing, wooing, laughing, crying
Sometimes things are very trying.

We all are lucky to have the smell
Of roses, lilac and the bluebell.
The garden is the place to be
Is it nearly time for tea?

*John Pierrepont*

## OUTSIDE CLIFTON POLYTECHNIC

Quietly over the valley, in the cool bright winter sun
I gaze through the frost-spiked branches of the trees,
the weight upon
them of the frozen dew and the snow,
Speaks of an absolute coldness, that only the dead can know.

Carefully through the valley the cluttered stream made its path
A river of life and comfort,
until it was frozen to death.
Now the ice is black and unyielding, and the river's flotsam is held
Paralysed in that coldness, that only the dead have felt.

As evening falls in the valley, gently covering the sounds
Even the sun has faltered
as it sought to make amends
For its failure, and now has retreated, falling with roseate gleam
Into the Stygian blackness, which only the dead have seen.

Yet somehow over the valley, an air of hope still prevails
The sun's return is expected,
a promise that never fails.
And even amidst the coldness of that frost-swamped winter's night
A bird-singing dawn is portended, in which only the living delight.

*Ray Smart*

# GLEN URQUHART

I want to go back to my glen in the spring
To savour the glories that place always brings.
The timeless hills and the endless sky,
The sky where buzzards float and cry.
If I climb to the top on tired aching legs,
There's an unafraid Dotterel guarding his eggs,
But the Ptarmigan shepherds her young ones to cover
She feels they are safer under the heather.
One memorable day I remember it yet
A mother Pine Martin passed by at my feet
As I watched, hardly breathing my wonderment grew
Three golden bibbed babies were passing by too.
On small secret lochs high up in the hills,
The gold crested Grebe are dashing about,
It's easy to see they are doing their best
Tending their damp improbable nest.
There in a hollow two hares box and dance
And lead me, still dancing away down the path.
Tumbling water cold down from the hills
The crack of a twig as a deer drinks her fill.
But Peewit's getting quite distressed
And tries to lure me from her nest.
So I'll walk away and head for home
Pondering on our wonderful world.

*Judy McEwan*

# WINTER BLOSSOM

Thro the hard soil, whitened by frosty fingers
The first snowdrops shyly raise their heads
Their delicate bell-shaped flowers modest
Fragile as a string of beads
Snowy-white petals gently mock the bitter weather
As they coyly spread their enchantment
To bewitch and delight those who wish to see
And marvel at the wonder of nature's ability
To create this exquisite tiny flower
Which grows and blooms in the cold, frosty weather

*Joan Hughes*

## TROUBLED ON EVERY SIDE

Troubled on every side, but not perplexed
Cast down, but not in despair
Do such sentiments fill today's air?
Indeed they do, but where, not out there?
For trouble does apply, so much day by day
And can we that fact deny?
For look around, can you hear that silent cry?
Does it bring from you, another sigh?
We hope to encourage our young folk today
We try to guide them as best we may
So where does it all go wrong, dare I say
When oh so many appear to go astray, sadly
We thought, mum, the you and I, they were not doing so badly
Then wham! They are suddenly in a jam, led indeed
Are they into it, like a lamb, but to the slaughter
Your son, yes! And your daughter
What more they ask, (some mums), can they offer,
Their young to more responsible be
It is in our very society, this sickness you see, say others
Should we more still educate? Or hand all they want,
Out to them on a plate
Somehow they go on, in spite of us, (the caring ones)
To seal their own fate, all far too young
By drugs and drink, whiles promiscuity, and also
Modernity stung, if you ask me
While the churches empty, silence there is heard
As outside, the world does sadly, but herd them away
Where is Christ, where is love, where is real security today,
Mothers and fathers, dare you pray, to God above?

*Margaret Lightbody*

## OUR WORLD

Surrounding, cosy, comforting world
Is evermore as it becomes unfurled.
The sand that nestles 'neath our feet,
The little lambs in spring that bleat.

There's nothing wrong with the world that surrounds,
The beauty is there, it's all around.
The leaves that fall in autumn's days,
We know that winter's next come what may.

A beautiful place in which to live and die,
For we know we'll have to say goodbye.
So we still struggle in strength and duty
To stay in this world of surrounding beauty.

Only man is out of sync
That's why he needs this beauty to drink.
To feed his mind with his surroundings clear
And in his heart to hold them dear.

*Denise Shaw*

## PRAYER FOR PEACE

I asked for peace, my sins arose, and bound me close
I asked for truth, I asked for love, in a world of
Plenty, and with their din, my doubts come in,
My sins arose I could not find release, they
Wearied all faith, and grieves assailed, within
Thy heart to be around, beneath, above, enlighten
With faith's light my heart inflame it with love
Fire: I shall not fear, the dark; and cold, are
War, Lord send a beam on me, ten thousand times
Ten thousand sound thy praises, but who am I?
A worm, brightness unto me while thy foot steps
Trace, a sound of God comes to my ears, with all
Fire and light, Lord, treasure up my mite thy
Knowledge is the only line thou art a sea with
Out a shore, a sun without a sphere; thy place
And power is everywhere.

*I Savage*

# NEAR WILDERN MEADOW

A day to truly find your friends
A day to sit outside
A day you dream will never end
These days will never die.
It's a time to slow yourself right down
To take in all you see,
To find yourself, just mellowed out
And everyone, and thing, is free.

Remembering the times gone by
And the smiles that we all shared.
The laughs we had on summer days
Where no one really cared
About the things that we had planned,
The things we meant to do,
When all our plans flew out the door
And vanished in the blue.

Oh I'll always remember
Days we spent in the sun.
And I never, ever, want to forget
The peace of being young.

*Paul Edwards*

## DATURA IN MOONLIGHT

A tall tree, overhung with flowers too bright to watch,
Long white blossoms swing in the morning wind.
Branches sway, heavy laden, tasselled with white horns
That fling fierce sunlight back to the day, shiny as ice fields.
They posture extravagantly in the heat, requiring to be admired.
Wind and sun ebb to an evening of quieter colours;
The tree breathes a scent of Arabian silks and stories.
Each elegant trumpet glows as only a white flower can at dusk,
Tipped and curled like medieval footwear at a court of kings.

In moonlight the datura tree comes into her own
Poised as a waterfall turned to stone, a graceful statue
Carved and Carrera sharp. Suspended bellmouthed flowers
Float under endless heights of star polished atmosphere.
Windless midnight hangs, a ball of blue spun glass:
A breath, a whisper, an arrogant thought will shatter it.
Heraldic flowers on a field azure
Outshine that power in the sky, the mountained moon.
Acknowledge the ivory empress of enchanted indigo night.

*Viv Eliz*

## OUR WORLD

Our surrounding world is in trouble,
With whirlwinds and earthquakes as such
Coming in the silence of night
Destroying many places with might
A frightening roar causing a fright
With homes flattened and properties
All strewn along the land
And also heavy rainfalls
Causing floods and land to subside
It's frightening to see all this
And we must find a way
To stop this happening some how
I'm sure they can some day.

*Margaret Eirlys Stumpp*

## THE WOODLANDS

How lovely the woods our heritage
To destroy these trees would be sacrilege
In spring we see fresh green shoots
Beneath the tree's strong growths of roots

In spring a carpet of snowdrops pure and white
Pale yellow primroses, what a glorious sight
Golden daffodils with lovely bright crowns
Amidst the wonderful greens and browns

Later on the beautiful bluebells we see
And in profusion there's the anemone
Little furry rabbits go running around
Enjoying their freedom without a sound

When the trees are decked with green
In their branches all kinds of birds are seen
They build their nests high in the tree
Then sing their songs so happily

There's great big oak trees spreading their arms
Lovely bushy firs with old world charms
Copper beeches, elms growing to a great height
These woodlands are a marvellous sight

*Elizabeth Mary Dowler*

## SPRING

Spring is here once more my love,
I see it, breath it, feel the soft warm rain
upon my face, as we walk this winding lane.
The celandines are there to greet us
as we walk hand in hand.
The catkins and pussy willows, the hedgerows
seem to whisper, 'Isn't life just grand.'
The birds are happy on the wing, singing their endless song,
their mating time is here once more, and
Mother Nature isn't long
telling all spring is here.
We hear the cheerful blackbird
up in a pear tree near,
singing its song, its special song
to welcome the time of year.
The sun comes out and o'er the fields
I see a rainbow.
A pot of gold some people say is planted there, somewhere.
We walk a little further on to where the old mill stands
like an ageing giant in the sky,
surrounded by daffodils.
Their golden trumpets, like one massive band
guarding this enchanted place, and
down below the gurgling waters in the brook
embrace the mossy stones as if to say,
'It's spring, it's here hooray.'
Up the hill and o'er the fields we walk.
Let's wait awhile and watch the lambs
frolicking as they play,
they run and jump as if to chase their cares away.
Oh God is good to give such wealth to all
who spends a little of our time;
Time, just to recall
It's spring again, yes spring.

*Margaret R Bevan*

# THE SMELL OF THE SEA

As I smelt the smell of the sea
Memories of childhood washed over me.
Of sand and shingle at the seaside
And breakwaters placed so evenly
Imposing the beach on the estuary.

Since then I've known shores with unbroken line
Stretching to infinity, with sand textured like flour
Without stones or shells, though you search by the hour.

Yet I long for the narrow shingled space
With the mud flats revealed as the water recedes at a pace.
Its return brings the scenes
Of breakwaters, slowly submerging like tired submarines.
Moored boats forlorn on their side
Then buoyantly bobbing in the thrusting tide.

The cry of the gulls and the splash of the waves
And the hurt of the shingle as you go down to bathe.
Memories of childhood lived by the sea
Forever, forever remain with me.

*Peter Sowter*

# FLYING SOUTH IN SEPTEMBER

Discreetly, small woodland, and garden birds have left.
Subtle differences are made in a mere week.
North Norfolk's village of Cley lures wheat ears
On feather-borne voyages to Iberia.
Waders from the north land there, too tired and weak

With wing-ache; they've come for the marshes and mud flats.
Seeds dropped by birds and animals many years
Ago, became trees now flown over by swallows

And their relatives, house martins and swifts follow
To where they always nest, in our hemisphere.
Despite harvest-ready fields, and leaves that stay
Mainly green, something uncanny warns them of winter.
Cool winds in feathers whisper, 'Fly, be on your way.'

*Gillian C Fisher*

## MUSIC FOR THE BIRDS

Piano notes drifted out from
the window into the garden long.
Local birds joyfully broke out
into song.
How they loved it when she
practised all her lovely tunes.
The robin puffed his deep red
breast and then fairly swooned.
Scornfully he watched the sparrows
trying to have a go, but they never
reached those high notes only the lows.
A lone seagull floated by watching
two gentle doves, but they were happy
just to sing of their eternal love.

Suddenly a fragile nightingale
joined in with all of them. The
other birds fell silent they felt
they were in heaven.

*J H McIntyre*

## SHADES OF SHORE

The ghosts of fishers lull the foam;
sea mists suggest they cloak marine
spectacular, this dream my home,
enticing and nostalgic scene,
once proud possessor of chain pier
long decades back as Brighthelmstone;
sea gulls like aspirations veer,
drama sovereigns weirdly moan
their wild allegiance to the brine;
pavilion, a fire of gold
caressed by seaside solar shine;
old pageantries to thrill unfold
and make imagination reel,
giddily fuelling atmosphere.
Now a mere visitor I feel
exhilaration to be here.
Amusement pushes time askance,
quietens as a band performs;
adored, delighted infants dance,
a scene my heart with spirit warms.
The painted characters leave frame,
come alive and embellish past
grubby canvasses with acclaim.
It seems some avid brush worked fast
such glowing tableau to reveal,
a walking, talking vivid oil,
can it possibly lose appeal
for me, again on Sussex soil?

*Ruth Daviat*

## THE SUN STILL SHONE

Whatever men did
The sun still shone
On that twenties-thirties land,
In easy days of summers
Before the chimes of war rang loud.

We laughed as we played
In fields, on hills,
Climbed mountains at Eastertime,
Held carnivals for village folk
With prizes for dress and rhyme.

There was excitement on trains
That sped joyful to sea for
Seagulls and sandwiches,
Pennies and rides,
With warm splashing waves
That could harm no child;

Till it was home again
Rubbing sand-tired eyes,
The noise of the day
Spinning round in one's mind
With memories of waves
And white bobbing sails -
Oh the sea and the sand
Which had been all ours!

*Rowland Ablett*

## THE CROWN OF THE NILE

Lake Victoria, is the crown of the Nile
   not just a large plain filled with rain,
it is not very deep, simply two hundred feet
   and has only one place it can drain.

This lake is quite large, as big as a sea
   and its temper is one to be seen,
it was found by a Brit not that long ago
   who named it for love of his Queen.

On the edge of the lake many minerals are found,
   such as diamonds, gold, silver and tin,
the bed of the lake is also quite rich
   where the minerals, by rain, have washed in.

There are islands with beaches as white as whipped cream,
   there are ships just as frequent as mail,
there are dugout canoes used in catching lake fish
   which are powered by an old lanteen sail.

Living islands that float made from reeds and tall grass
   full of crocs, large snakes and such things,
some islands are large and move with the wind
   with mosquitoes that have a big sting.

On the west of the lake, large estates have been made
   growing coffee and tea and much fruit,
the east side is dry where the cotton is grown
   where wild animals are illegal to shoot.

This great inland lake formed by an earth's surface fault
   is the catchment of Egypt's lifeline,
nearly four thousand feet above the Red Sea
   it is fresh and free from all brine.

When the wet season's on, it rises four feet,
   all twenty-six thousand square miles,
then it gushes away and floods down the Nile,
   little wonder the Sphinx often smiles.

*Les Cwmrod*

# A QUEEN OF BEAUTY

The bloom was black and deepest blue,
Its centre purest gold,
Its petals widely radiate,
A glory to behold.

Its fragrance was a perfume that
Enchantment was to breathe.
Minor blooms were round it spread,
And velvet moss beneath.

A very Queen of Beauty, high
Above the garden's norm -
It made my spirit reverent by
Perfection of its form.

*Henry Harding Rogers*

## CONTRASTS

Mountains stark and barren stand -
Covered by purest snow, so grand
Tree roots gnarled, branches bent,
Attacked by raging winds are rent.
Hardly anyone's intruded -
On this landscape so secluded.
Lonely eagles soar on high
Where stormy clouds go scudding by.

Through gravest need the birds have come
Hunting for food to feed their young.
Even in this hostile place
A tiny wild flower lifts its face.
Spring starts to decorate with care
Rocks that previously were bare.
Snows that melting downwards flow
Watering earth and plants below.

Deep down in sheltered spots are seen
Grasses of the brightest green.
Soon all the countryside is blessed
With vibrant colours richly dressed.
Longer, warmer pleasant hours -
Soon winter's icy grip o'er powers.
Clothed in such a fine array
Tells of summer, on the way.

We're all aware there is a reason
For these changes of the season.
Night following day and sun, the rain
Joy comes to cheer us after pain.
Man needs faith and eyes to see
How wonderful this world can be.
Surrounded by God's love and care
He's with us always, everywhere.

*Joan Carr*

# EARTH AND SKY

Weird mushroom clouds
twist up from earth to sky
ooze bulbous growths of wrath
with chink lit eye -

Flash streaks of light
down spire and turret tiles
while ghoulish fiends
stir darkness sparked with guile -

As eerie dusk bats swoop
sparred fox slinks home
and owl tucks into nook
war's thrust explodes -

Dark thunder roars
and tumbled powers fall
but earth is quenched
her lust for life recalled.

*Rosemary Keith*

## HOMESPUN TRUTHS

The sky is a brilliant blue with no cloud in sight,
The east wind has blown itself out so all is calm, all is quiet,
The trees are at rest - hardly a twig moves - no leaves as yet
But below the park, hidden by the steep side, is a yellow shrub.
The gorse peeps out, ignoring the cold, waving its barbs,
Daring people to touch it - sharper than rose thorns.
The mountain range, is covered with ice, having let in the New Year.
But to me it's too near, too stark, so clear crevices are seen
And foretells rain, despite the calm sea in the bay and all its beaches.
It's one of many things I learnt, as a child, in the countryside.
Lately the sky at night has been a gorgeous blood-coloured red,
Signifying that the next day will be sunny and cloudless
Whereas red sky in the morning is 'shepherds warning' and ours,
Often meaning there will be rain before nightfall ends.
There's so much to learn on this patch of Britain.
It's Welsh through and through, much older than the Romans
Who came, saw and conquered from The Rivals to Bardsey.
The Romans killed everyone who fought for their beloved country
So its secrets in its history, frequently shrouded in mist
And more often than not the media's weather 'forecast' is wrong.
Llyn 'unrecognised' because Scotland and Ireland are preferred
But I put my trust in the Welsh predictions and myths.

*Tilla B Smith*

## THE WALK

Like angels singing in the distance,
   church bells sing out their morning song.
Each peal fills my heart with contentment,
   as I slowly walk along.

A country lane stretches before me,
   high hedges obstruct my view.
The smells of nature are all around,
   this is a paradise clean and new.

The lane now meets a main road,
   there are fields as far as the eye can see.
Here farmers grow the crops,
   that feed towns' people like you and me.

Two miles from the nearest village,
   enjoying this natural scenery.
A herd of cows grazing in the sun,
   taking sustenance from the greenery.

Houses appear on the horizon,
   my walk is almost at an end.
Still looking at the beauty around me,
   my heart knows it has found a new friend.

Entering the small village,
   I turn to take just one look.
My eyes admire God's creation,
   my mind wonders at the patience it took.

*M A Challis*

## OUR DAILY LIFE

Go and fill the kettle
I would like a cup of tea.
Where do I get the water from?
Can't you see?

Just turn the tap and let it flow
The water is alright
It makes a lovely cup of tea
The plug is at your right.

Oh, do you need the light as well?
No, not yet, we don't need it
I mean the current of power
Which heats the water in it.

What magic you have got to use
It's like another world
What brain the people have,
To learn and understand.

Yes, light and gas and water
And many, many more
The telephone, the music
The television now.

We are surrounded by our thoughts
To use the world around us
But it's the will we have to use
To live our life in comfort.

Don't be deceived by the fact
That we are well advanced
It is the effort we must use
To keep up our stance.

*Elisabeth Anna*

## PRIMROSES

The way is sometimes long and dark
But hark,
The angels voices sing
And primroses shall greet the spring

These gentle flowers, so pure, so sweet,
Unfold with joy and deep delight -
Bring happiness to searching eyes
While blessings fall from winter skies.

By streams and banks their tiny star
Brings a joyful message from afar -
And though the world is dark and cold
This hope wells up from days of old

For each morn day follows night
And everywhere is God's own light
The Lord of Nature guides our way
And shields our footsteps every day.

*Marcella Pellow*

## COMING HOME

I came in on the branch line,
The blackened end of platform six,
That cold, chafed haze
Of being home not fully
Understood, of knowing
That tomorrow might just
As simply see me leave,
A presence noted, not
Quite missed.

So was this really where
It all began; the trimmed, tight
Streets, the brass-eyed doors,
Windows like pint glasses
With a head of lace;
The dusty webs of coal house sheds,
Lean-to where we oiled black bikes
For chasing girls on Sunday rides?

Was it here that we strode
Out, heads in air, the new found
Lads about our common town,
Then separated all too soon
To regiments and pitted war?

But here, the blackened
End of platform six, it all
Looks much the same, much
As before, if that is what
An overdue, long-promised
Coming home is for.

*Brian Parvin*

## WHAT GAIN?

What gain have we, should all the world be ours,
And moral justice our endeavour's hope,
Should we have no conception of the truth,
Nor could not see beyond ambition's scope?

What freedom has our spirit, should we bind,
Mind's concept to authoritarian rule,
What chance to blend and permeate the whole,
Should we ourselves not see, as nature's fool?

What price to raise the curtain on the past,
To bind old hurts and grievance to our soul,
What happiness to cast away the dross,
And be as one in love's united goal?

What chance to mould the future of the world,
Within the grasp of every beating heart,
Who gazing on the error bred within,
Discards then makes a new conserted start.

Surveying life you may perchance to see,
That lessons of the past, were dearly bought,
And destiny determined by the mass . . .
Who blundered in the concept of truth's thought.

Rise up above the chains that bind the soul,
Be free from error's grasp, it but degrades,
The outer and the inner not at one,
The plight of man throughout time's lost decades.

What pleasure should each mind retain the thought,
That life's evolvement was its duty's aim,
And progress forge ahead in name of truth,
And in whose concept all may 'future' gain!

*Marie McCreanor*

## THE WINTER LAKE

The lake in all its wintery delight
Silvery shadows with icy white
How still it seems; I gaze in awe
Inhaling the frost and wanting more.

The lake has such a sparkling glow
As the sky leans over lending snow.
Like soap drifting down from up high
Cleaning the trees as they softly sift by.

The lake has a glistening gleaming glow
Pale swans silently glide over the frosty snow
Freezing cold water hidden beneath
A shimmering shapely wintery sheath.

The lake, coy seduction upon her face
Surroundings trimmed with snowflake lace.
Now the sun peeps down in orange glory
Soaking up this celestial story.

*Linda Hurdwell*

## AURORA

Crescent moon swings low and waits
to catch a falling star, chill
stings face, tears glisten eyes
upraised and memories chase
shadows in the evening still.
Time travels snowscape's purity,
hamlets enshrouded hushed pass by,
sky wrinkled fierce and ruling land laid
flat, trees stunted in winds raging.
Ice freezes breath and taste, skin dry,
head aches through fleecy covering.
New moon scythes clouds, Aurora glows
bright circles swirling Arctic frost,
with mirror image forming high above
Antarctic lands. Rich colour flows
an emerald panoply, enlivening horizons dark.
Power from Creator's loving hands, scintillates
in autumn, spring, fire flashing, twisting
out of amber heart, alluring man long
journeying, each devotee most humbly waits.
Borealis and Australis, Aurora, goddess of
the dawn, charging earthward, magnetising
paths alight for newlyweds and those
prospecting gold. Celestial blaze since life
began, rainbow streaking, harmonising
heavenly courts with earth below. Time
travels slow, home beckoning in evening's hush,
tears glisten eyes, face soft in welcome warmth,
moon rises memories breathtaking far, somewhere
wings flurry light horizons dark, as angels rush.

*Lorna Troop*

## TO A ROBIN

O neat little bird - you're there in the tree,
　　Perched on a bare branch.
I hear your magic and strain to see
　　Your tiny form.

Your rapturous notes, melodious trills
　　And glorious tunes
Float down to me, when the cold wind chills,
　　And bring me warmth.

You delicate bird - so small and so shy,
　　You take all my breath.
I wallow entranced as I swallow a sigh
　　From deep inside.

O creature of song, tell the world to be still,
　　To hear in your voice
The glory of living, and share in the thrill
　　Of a song that will always rejoice.

*Marj Norton*

## MIRROR-LAND

We look in mirrors
To seek the truth, but waters
Flow much softer there.

Somebody will take my hand
To quiet places we will go
On the far side of the mirror-land.

Far from this world's noisy band
Where life is good and life is slow
Somebody will take my hand

Where willow breezes gently fan
On lazy rivers we might row
On the far side of the mirror-land

Or walk along some drifting sand
Where shifting waters ebb and flow
Somebody will take my hand

A life together we'll have planned
And cottage gardens I will show
On the far side of the mirror-land.

I need escape my troubles, and
If I stay here they'll surely grow.
Somebody will take my hand
On the far side of the mirror-land.

*Audrey Preston*

## THE 4 HORSEMAN...

There is a fearful plague today
Rolling through this lovely world
Making all of us afraid
Evil anger and greed unfurled.

There is a dreadful famine now
That cannot be contained
Have we left it too late again?
Oh come don't look so pained!

There are a hundred wars going on
Right around this planet
It won't get out of hand will it?
Will we keep the bomb or ban it?

The fire of evil in our hearts
That spread without a break
Brings envy drug abuse despair
Neglect and abortion cause our hearts to quake.

Wake up and ask yourselves this question
How much longer can the nations wait
Deliberately debasing love and truth
Ask God yes He is still in date!

*Petronilla Cockin*

## THE COUNTRYSIDE

Fields and fields for miles around.
From mountains and valleys and down to the ground.
The silence is golden and air is so sweet,
With water so pure it goes down a treat.
The forests are green and hedges are too,
The rivers are clear and skies are so blue.

Down in the valley, did you ever know?
The deep waters cry and white water's flow.
The animals and insects gather to feast,
As torture is gone and pain is deceased.
There are foxes and birds and some deer too,
This peace and tranquillity is simply not true.

This could be helpful from time spent by you,
Let's start up new life where old things once grew.
Don't throw your litter on the side of the road,
And don't leave your rubbish where rivers once flowed.

Planting new plants and growing new trees,
Could make a difference for some birds and bees.
Respect the countryside as it may not be there,
If we take its beauty and then strip it bare.

*Barry Busby*

## EVERGREEN

Life's turbulence calms
   with the green of the forest
The balance of nature
   remains evergreen.

Wars ravish the earth
   yet all of its horrors
The hand of time heals
   and creates a new scene.

The technology of man
   is another abrasive
And countryside lost
   in a new war of speed

But time marches on and
   God in His Mercy
Will restore Mother Nature
   to offset man's greed!

*Mary Skelton*

## TIDE TURN IN CHAUSEY

Minute white waves - weak kitten's claws
Bend, breaking, beach-bound.
Fast flowing downward water
Wind-whipped. Meeting
Inexorable tidal flow.
Islands - imagined? - banished.
Sea swung shelving shoals
Consumed, content to lie below.

Wind meeting tide - the boat -
Stirs from her lazy lethargy.
Meets motion, raft renewed.
Along the vanishing shore
Grey gulls, gusty, plod and pout.
Silver shoals, sea driven, circle
And leap. Push perilously upward
Whilst petrol-powered people race about.

A cabin cruiser, topsy tipped by shallow sand
Lies listing, waiting water for her cure.
A fishing boat beach-stranded,
Deck rolls her latent lobster pots.
In the sunset, little dwellings
Cluster round rude rocks, soon to be sea.
Killed craft, sad skeletons sit -
Watching water which will now submerge
Wind-wasted timbers. Whilst the summer sky
Wing-filled, shines soft above the surge.

*Jean Rhodes*

## RAINBOW

After the sun came the showers
In the stream I saw waters flow.
Pouring over pretty flowers
And now I see a big rainbow.

On the other side I've been told
I could find some hidden treasure.
Some silver or a pot of gold
Hidden amongst deep green heather.

I see the dewfall on the hills
As its sparkle catches my eye
And through the rocks the water spills
All underneath the sun-drenched sky.

A moment like this is so rare
With mosaic colour in the air.

*Paul McIntyre*

## A VIBRATION

Ethical Egdon most rare of breed,
Those that draw near you must accept your creed.
Still, churches came here and there
Awakening within your barrows an enlightening.
Shaking shades of green bestir upon you,
The golden lights of gorse pave the way true.

Your cross of silver, roads only a Roman knows,
Heather the colour of purple Tyre he chose.
He could not holden to your heathen ways
Left he did, left you to your mutterings.
Farms sprang up, miles between sienna,
Men's pittance was parasang forever.

Then, then a cincinnatus came to cinture you,
A knight to stride your silver cross, adieu.
There had to be to your mesmerism,
A fight was on and so shall it be.
That golden head that flashed by
You knew was a match for your mauve eye.

So, you abided your time, seasons came and went,
At last this quiet roaring Godlike sons time was spent.
No, not the heat-hazed desert, or cold seas
Or aerial catastrophe galore
Could send him to unknown oblivion,
Excepting you, he knew that! brooding Egdon!

*L P P*

## OUR SURROUNDING WORLD . . .

To touch an emaciated body of a Third World child
Is mysterious beyond all telling.
The touch is like touching a new-born lamb
All light and fluffy
How precious the enfant . . .
To taste the cool mountain springs
Of the Appalacian Mountains.
The taste refreshes and intoxicates the spirits
To see the vast open landscapes of Russia
And admire their eternal youth
You appreciate their awe-inspiring beauty.
To listen to a chaffinch upon a bough
Relaying melodies to young and old
It does indeed lift a drooping spirit.
To smell the evergreens of the Black Forest
Perfumed like the sands of Arabia
Oh how beautiful the inspiration of the *senses*
It delights the soul in all of us . . .

***Rita Cleary***

## WINTER WOOD

The smell of dank, decaying leaves, invades your nostrils
Mud oozes, squelching with each single step
Brittle crack, as long-dead twigs succumb beneath your tread
Lichen clings, to trees, moss to rotting stumps
Lacy cobwebs drape from leafless branches, hopefully
Their creators, watching, waiting to pounce
On unsuspecting insects, that just might come their way
The horizon between nut bush and tree
Hazy white, moisture filled wraiths of mist,
Weave their silent swirls in the still damp air
Overhead, the trees thrust bare branches to the sky
They touch, breaking the soft silence beneath
Squirrels scuttle feverishly along branches,
As though the hounds of Hell were on their tails
Magnificent isolation, yet deep in its heart,
It holds a warm promise of things to come
Below in winter slumber, the spring flowers lie cocooned
Buds on bare branches swell with bright green hope
But for now we squelch in mud-soaked leaf mould, through the mist
Winter woods hold their own magnetic charm.

*Dora Watkins*

## MY SILENT WORLD

I am flesh and blood and throbbing veins
Beating heart, ageing complaints.
I am one who sees the myriads of colours bright
And welcomes seasons grateful for the gift of sight.

I can delight in the smell of new-mown grass
Coffee beans, baking bread and flowers en masse
Each morn I awaken with an optimistic feel
Of what treasures, hopes, this day will reveal.

I look closely at the sky
The grass, the flowers, the birds that fly.
Waves excite me with their roll
The rippled sand and green seaweed mould.

Traffic and great activity
Just part of life, I look and see.
I hear no sounds at all but have no difficulty with recall
An ageing process so they say
I have no complaints,
For most of life I had it all.

*Gloria Hargreaves*

## ST CYRUS

Ah, the little path, sand-drifted,
With all round, in summer, pink thrift
Bobbing and dipping in the short turf,
And below,
On the jewel-bright sea,
White sails skipping.

The little path, shell-strewn,
Where now, in winter,
Dried grasses lift and sway,
And below,
Under a pewter sky,
The dull surf beats in an empty bay.

*Mary Kalugerovich*

## SUFFOLK LANDSCAPE

Poppies flash a scarlet red across this Suffolk field,
Ripening wheat lies in-between, its harvest soon to yield,
Dusk it is approaching, mist lies in the glow,
The sun sinks ever-slowly - what majesty to show,
Maybe this is Flanders or Ireland's Emerald Isle?
Suffolk with its beauty retains a certain style.
Poppies flash a scarlet red, bow heads to meet the night,
Showing Suffolk's glory as bird's wing dusky flight.

*W Curran*

## FIVE SENSES - OR NON-SENSES

Eyes that see the world and yet see nothing:
sunsets painted on an evening sky,
spring blossom white and heavy on the trees,
blue summer skies far bluer than the sea,
autumn colours rich in bronze and gold
and winter magic 'neath a veil of snow . . .
eyes that see it all and yet see not
the needs of fellow men.

Ears that hear the world and yet hear nothing:
minuets of springtime in the trees,
lullabies of summer in the fields,
notes of music playing crystal-clear,
water rippling in a mountain stream,
echoes in the hills and in our lives . . .
ears that hear it all and yet hear not
the needs of fellow men.

Men who smell the sea and yet smell nothing:
the salty tang that lingers in the air,
forest fern, pine trees in the copses,
woodland flowers, scent of summer roses,
home-baked bread, aroma of fresh coffee . . .
men who smell the earth smell not
the squalor and the anguish of the homeless,
the needs of fellow men.

Hands that feel and touch and yet feel nothing,
that mould and shape the form of things to come:
the richness of brocade and of gold thread,
the gloss of satin in a bridal gown;
smoothness of cold marble and a pebble,
velvet leaves and sponginess of moss . . .
hands that feel and touch and yet feel not
the needs of fellow men.

Tongues that taste and try and yet taste nothing:
subtle flavours full of mystery,
sweet and sour from the orient,
mild and bitter mixed in harmony,
herbs and spices from exotic lands
and mellow wine matured and ripe with age . .
tongues that taste and try but never fill
the needs of hungry men.

**Suzanne Low Steenson**

## ON THE SHORE

*(Written on Age Concern holiday at Redcar
with visits to Saltburn-by-the-Sea and Seaton Carew)*

If I left my bed at dead of night
What should I find on the frenzied shore?
Bones of seagulls, carcass of whale,
Terror of wind and a sodden sail?

Leaping and lashing, pulling my feet,
Tearing, towering, crushing heart's beat,
Breathless, timeless, horror of night,
No one, nothing, to witness my plight!

Wake, O awake from trauma and fear,
See dawn's dancing in colours so clear;
Ripple of lace-edge, call of the gull,
Peace and solace my soul to fill.

*Irene J Grainger*

## MESSENGERS OF LOVE!

I woke one day to bright sunlight,
And as I watched the birds in flight,
I wondered why God gave them wings?
I watched them as they soared on high,
A tiny speck in a vast blue sky,
And suddenly my heart began to sing.

Of course I'd read it in the Holy Book,
For from the Ark one flew to look,
For a land God meant for them to dwell.
And there was the snow-white Dove,
Chosen by God, the symbol of love,
Bringing peace to Man on earth as well.

Then there are His Angels who guard us while we sleep,
To protect us from all evil, their silent vigil keep,
That we might rise refreshed to face another day.
With this knowledge I now understand,
A few were chosen by His Hand,
To carry to Man the love He sends our way.

*M Muirhead*

## STAND

Stand and smell the roses,
the tulips and buttercups fair.
Touch the breeze which flows,
cross the summer's cleansing air.

Stand and see creation
in all its radiance bright,
taste the crystal stream's fountain,
hear the sweet owls coo this night.

Stand upon Heaven's pasture,
created for woman and man,
try to find such euphoric splendour
anywhere else - if you can!

The glory of God surrounds us,
a sure blessing for all to see.
To smell, to touch, to taste,
the cup from Heaven's vineyard tree.

Stand and raise your praises,
give thanks on a bended knee.
This glory and this creation,
was bestowed lovingly to you and me.

*Steve Kettlewell*

## LONE DEAD GUM

In almost every field, backyard or lot
you'll find at least one gum tree,
gaunt, silver-grey, naked, dead,
its topmost brittle branches
like the rigid claw-like fingers
of a corpse half-buried on the battlefield
thrusting insensible to a rising sun.
A paradigm of Nature's work plan,
the inexorable cycle of life and death.

But when you see a lone dead gum,
the *only* tree, dead or living,
in the middle of an open field,
paradoxically this wraith-like form
exudes a powerful presence;
no longer a symbol of death-in-life
but rather life-in-death.
And when at sunset the lone gum
stands silhouetted against a blood-red sky,
its ghostly branches reaching out
like the desperate imploring hands
of tormented souls in Hell,
it looms portentous, darkly brooding,
one of Nature's ever-watchful sentinels.

*Ray Wilson*

## THE FIVE SENSES OF TRUE LOVE
*(Dedicated to my husband, Pat)*

To breathe in each familiar smell,
Which only in his virile form dwell,
Manly, musky, erotic, alluring,
My lifetime love for him enduring.

His warm breath, the touch of his skin
From this man, who is totally masculine.
His tender fingertips as they explore,
Thrill me now even more than before.

Sparkling, mischievous, still boyish eyes.
Continue to captivate mine, tantalise,
Muscular hairy legs, powerful, strong,
Wrapped round mine, where they belong.

The taste of his lips, with mine combine,
Sweeter than the ripest fruit of the vine.
With our bodily juices mingling as one,
Our thirst is quenched, all aridness gone.

His quick wit makes me laugh out loud,
He is my best friend, for which I am proud,
Of whom I hold the deepest respect,
Admiring him for his sharp intellect.

This man brings all my five senses alive,
Helping me on life's journey to survive.
After thirty-tree years of married life,
I am delighted that I am his wife.

***Janet Hewitt***

## NATURE'S WILD DISPLAY

Tiny harbour, oh so small,
Seldom sees a boat.
Now, upon this wild spring tide
Nothing is afloat.
High waves break upon the wall
Along the harbour's side.

Dark waves surging, greenly-grey;
Oh what loud reports:
Again, again, like cannon's roar
Wind an wave retorts.
Towering waves fling high white spray
Upon the Cornish shore.

Again there comes another crash
As wall and rocks with wild water clash.
Exalt at Nature's wild display
Upon this windy day.

*Frances Joan Tucker*

## THE STORM

Oh dramatic skyline steeped with clouds
Above a lonely scene bereft of crowds
Should thunder ever find its voice
And crack loudly in this land of savage choice.

The sky surrendering rain upon the earth,
Teasing it, tempting it to show its worth.
Daring the ground to give up its meagre green
In scrappy, spindly plants so seldom seen.

Time divided into light and sound
All things alive are huddled underground.
As wind whips around the tortured rocks
And sets them trembling with the aftershock.

Granite cliffs pointing to the sky,
Above a wild dark sea that lashes high.
Electric currents riding on the air
Set unwary souls afire without a care.

*Jeannette Jones*

# SENSES AND MEMORIES

I remember primroses in far off woodland glades.
Rosettes so sweetly smelling, in sunlight and in partial shade.
Perfume delicately rising, up to meet the day,
A perfume that is but memory to me, and in a way,
Even more precious than it was right then.
A blessed gift of nature I may never know again.

I remember wading through sparkling bubbling streams,
Balancing on stepping stones, and dreaming far off dreams.
And watching speckled trout as they basked on riverbed,
While calling birds in spirals wheeled way above my head,
Singing their sweet songs and chirruping to the world.
Perfume may be lost, but sounds can still be heard.
I remember well, the sound of wind through the trees.
Of watching painted butterflies as they surf the summer breeze;
And I enjoy the happy sound of children at their play,
As they chase those dandelion fairies and wend their way
To pick some flowers I smell no more.
And, full circle, evens out the score.

*Jean Rosemary Regan*

## MY PEACE

A warm calming breeze
Sweeping in from the sea
My mind, is just drifting
The pleasures there for me.

To take away the hassles
The worry and the strife
To let you see the beauty
Of all the good things in life.

The Lord's beauty will unfold
As your eye's begin to see
All the gorgeous surroundings
Our Lord gave to you and me.

Hear the rush in the air
Let the slight feeling flow
Drift into imagination
Your troubles to let go.

All these calm surroundings
The feelings so good inside
A smile comes to your face
Your happiness you cannot hide.

If only it could last
Our life today, says no
But I know deep inside
For happiness, it's the place to go.

*Rob Passmore*

## OCEAN CHARM

Sat in a city
The ocean I crave
The smell on the breeze
Of salt, sand and wave.

Bladderack singles
And lying in strands
Making a mess
On pure golden sands.

Memories vivid
Of coastal retreats
Flash through my mind
As I meander dull streets.

Childhood adventures
Of fishing rockpools
The hunt for the blenny
Amidst shrill seagull calls.

Walking the summer
On cliffs rugged and proud
A clear place for thinking
Away from the crowd.

Still in the city
My mind is refreshed
With thoughts of my homeland
Cornwall. The best!

*Andrew Tatam*

## THE BEAUTY OF NATURE

The sense of touch and warmth,
The sense of hearing and rhythm,
The sense of sight and sheer delight,
The sense of smell and images,
The sense of taste and enjoyment,
Wrapped together, in our persona,
Who will value them, who will nurture them to advantage?
Who will gradually let them?
'Tis always easier to lose than to win,
It is not as easy to stay awhile and think.

Savour the sound of the sea, with all its changes, as in life,
Sometimes angry sometimes calm
Sometimes unapproachable another time tranquillity.
Hear the mighty waves pounding the rocks
Or see the gulls, struggling to catch their food.
Take a walk over the shore, always different
Sometimes, frenzied with sharp-edged rocks and broken mussel shells,
Another time, just bumpy rounded pebbles, later changing to cool,
                                        cool seaweed.
Followed by silky sand, softly caressing bare feet.
Taste the gentle salty breeze, the sun sinks on the horizon,
                                    then moonlight
Plays shadows on the shore, whilst a winged seabird glides
                                   across quietly,
Under heavenly stars, magnifying our senses.

*Joy Townsley*

## CORNISH MIST

As the waves lash the seashore
Hitting the rocks with powerful force
Puffins, guillemots, seabirds
     cling to the ledges
As sprays cascade.
     onto rocks off Land's End.
A place full of mystery - intrigue
     beckons to you, smugglers' haunts.
Listen to the seafaring tales,
     over cold ale.
Tell of bygone days.
Rugged coastline,
Dark dank caves,
Hidden shipwrecks.
Watch the tide,
White horses, that hit the seashore.
So much to see and explore
As evening shadows fall
Along a blustery harbour wall.
Phantom shadows - muffled whispers
Pirates from a distant past maybe?
As cold sea waves crash the shoreline.

*Margaret Parnell*

# SHUNYATA

The kiss of the Spirits make restless
weeping willow branches trailing
as Blessings from dark depths
ripple the sparkling surface
speaking of Light contained within
silver-green Angel hair drifts in recognition
across the water
whispering thoughts
while roots delve into the
Lifeblood of Earth and Water
fired by the Sun caressed
by sighing on the breeze
which shall be rested by the Moon
where reflections cast shadows
into the deep, deep, deep
releasing Light
while etched into crevices of the outer-bark
protecting patterns hold veins
where sap flows
by the pond where all comes together
Body, Spirit, Mind.

And the pendulum of the dandelion floats proclaiming
the Passage of Time.

*Anita Richards*

## THE MILKMAN

Clutching dear the slippery bottles,
the frail creature in canvas coat
sidled around the back of the truck,
tottering a little in his weariness -
sucking in the winter chill
and exhaling in great billows of condensation.

Coughing politely to clear irritating mote,
the trusty and true flat-back lorry
purred, and carried its master
to the next delivery,
a ravelled beanie his only insulation.

*Perry McDaid*

## MY ABUNDANT FRIEND

Standing through the seasons of life and giving off a scented aroma
from a profusion of blossom that arouses my senses.

A friend bearing fruits with a colour to match any morning horizon
or the setting of an orange sun, succulent and fresh as the morning dew
yet crisp in its shape ripe in its scent, with a taste of more to come,
firm in its form to the touch of my hand until the last has gone.

Then the leaves fall to touch the ground and the snow will come and go
so I wait, anxious for the blossom to reappear, so that in the warmth of
the sun I can again hold the abundance of fruit from my friendly
apple tree.

*John Barker*

# A WINTER WALK

An isolated old farmhouse near a disused railway line.
Surrounded by chalk-white fields of crispy snow.
Bare branches of the trees shiver beneath their unfriendly cloak.
Fences and hedges guard against footprints in the nearby field.
Telegraph poles standing and challenging the hostile conditions.
No sound to be heard, but crunching footsteps along the icy track.
Sun setting in the misty sky bringing an almost cosy feeling.
Aeroplane trails in the wintry sky, families flying to sunshine
and warmth.

*Katie Townsend*

## IN PRAISE OF ORCHESTRA

Tracing a sunlit valley through a shady glen,
Where thoughts and feelings marry, uniting once again;
Responsive to the heart, which like a flower unfolds
To gather up a part of what the music holds.

Soft whispered chords that pluck a vibrant string,
Reply to trumpet's taunt and oboe's carolling;
Hollow sounding bass effects a steadying note,
A mellowing tone upspringing from an ever-husky throat.

The horns re-echo sadly to hear the loud bassoon
And the thundering drum is silent, as if it spoke too soon;
The anguish of the harp, lives in the pulsing soul
Like an ever-singing harmony where thirsty waters roll.

The studied cadence of the flute whispers to fond delight;
Muted strings no longer stir, unequal to the fight.
The clarinet takes up the strain, limpid, cool, he wakes
The strings to new endeavour; mounting till there breaks

An avalanche of sound: With passionate embrace
To suffuse the listening ear with an ever-quickening pace;
Rising to crescendo, till the very air is still,
And all the Earth is silent, held, in the music's will.

Then of a sudden fades, and leaves no mark:
The drama of the moment, caught in a transient spark;
The chattering cymbal's clatter, bell-like and fancy free,
And the fickle cornet's patter; is a fading memory.

The hollow-throated answer that the sickly tuba gives,
Is echoed by the piccolo; to the timpani it lives;
Rousing from its slumber the saddened cor anglais,
To play her choicest psalmody with ever-wistful gaze.

So breaks sweet music on the sullen soul;
Each voice a part of one harmonious whole.

*Noelle M Hill*

## A LAKELAND SCENE

From the still, serene lake surface
The fell behind rises majestically
Up to crags covered with ice-like lace
Curtains shrouding them so mysteriously.

Small birds, duck, moorhen and coot
Feed in the shallow, lakeside harbour,
While I move closer in order to shoot
Off some film to record their strange behaviour.

Calls from these and other birds passing in the air
Mingle with the lapping sounds of the wavelets,
Bringing a soothing effect to all who are there
Which helps to take away the various causes of stress.

Up comes the sun over a distant hill,
Bathing the lakeside scene in its golden light.
Soon the frost melts away except for that still
Hidden in the shadows and out of its sight.

The sun's golden rays are reflected from ice far above
Giving the impression of lights twinkling and shining,
To be seen and felt just like God's radiant love
By all who would reflect on His glory this morning.

All this beauty can only have been created and arranged
By the hand of a God so loving and good.
Artists of every sort want scenes like this recorded
In oils and watercolours as well as the written word.

*Paul W Fleming*

# THE SEA

Dragging my feet through the bronzed stained sand,
Stained with the memories of my childhood.
The white water lapping at my feet,
Like a dog, which never leaves his owner.

But I am the dog, chasing the water
Chasing the recollections of my past
So long ago when I played as a child in the surf.

The ocean is calling, crying my name,
But I am its only listener,
Its one true friend,
And it, my companion,
Still waits for me.

And my reflection, still
So clearly displayed in the water.
My cheeky grin, my muddy face
And my rosy young cheeks
Still live in me,
Still live in the water.

Who knows what will become of me?
What will become of these memories?
Nor the place I loved,
The place I still love.

I sit and draw in the sand.
A stick rests in my palm,
As I carve away into the land,
Leaving my mark,
My signature.
Till the water comes and
Engulfs it in its path.

*Chloé Sharrocks  (14)*

## OCEAN'S MOTION

The grass-swept field a fluid motion resembling crests atop the ocean,
When wind blew gently 'pon my face and led the grass heads in a race.
I stopped to watch this lovely scene, the field bedecked in gold
and green.
Its undulating crest an unseen hand brushed 'pon its surface to move
the land.
This place was mine now for a while, I gently stepped down from
the stile,
I strolled amid the ocean's roots, dismayed to note the trail from boots.
I had to onward displace my sea to reach my home distant from me.
The grasses sighed to feel my feet, crushing the beauty I'd chanced
to meet.
Regrets came crashing through my heart at the ocean's ruin I'd had
to impart.
I looked back to note the damage done and thought to reduce it
with a run.
So fast now sped my legs, their stride intent to make the
footsteps wide.
Less damage was my sole desire, for not one blade to hurt so dire.
Now near my goal the furthest stile I'd run most nearly one half mile
But wait, my ocean was not done, the damaged lessened by my run.
I'd had to speed across the roots and in the process lost my boots
But yet I'm here to tell the tale though not again that field travail.

*Channon Cornwallis*

# PHOTOGRAPHING FOXGLOVES

I looked down the lens and
The foxglove drew me in
I felt like a bee
Sucked into the cool soft interior.

Pollen tickled my nose
My knees were covered in pollen
Soft summer drowsiness
Surrounded me.

Sun filtered pink
Cool cavern welcome
Spring business buzziness
My hair prickled -
The camera clicked.

***Charmian Goldwyn***

# As

As steady as my sister - as pink as a rose,
As fat as my brother - as rough as a bear,
As strong as an elephant - as weak as a bird,
As heavy as a chair - as light as pin,
As wet as a dolphin - as soft as a dog
As tight as my coat - as free like a baby.

*Bernice Rumble*

## SEASONS

The tall trees stand stark against the winter sky,
As icy wind drives the snow to scurry and fly.
For any creature to venture out would be folly,
Small birds seek shelter in the ivy or the holly.

Soon milder weather prompts the snow to retreat,
As new-born lambs call mother with constant bleat.
From icy bed, snowdrops give a first sign of spring,
Encouraging the winter-weary birds to forage and to sing.

Crocus and forsythia appear clear and startling bright,
Followed by a host of daffodils, creating a precious sight.
Easter winds dry out the soil to harrow and to till,
When farmers hasten with seed, and their busy drill.

Sunlit blossoms blaze against dark squall clouds passing,
On every tree and bush new emerald leaves are massing.
Nature's cycle has nothing so enchanting as the spring,
Filling one's soul full of joy, and one's heart to sing.

Summer comes quietly with her warm salad days,
Silent growth bursting 'neath the lazy shimmering haze.
Birds labour to feed their young's ever-open throats,
While watching out for the thieving magpie or the stoats.

The fruits have filled, and the corn stands full and ripe,
Meadows are lush, and the fledglings have taken flight.
The harvest starts with long dusty back breaking weeks,
Cutting and carting, man and his machine hardly sleeps.

The tranquillity of autumn comes with soft nights chilled,
Prayers of thanksgiving are said for barns that are filled.
Nature takes her winter sleep while windswept branches swing
The tall trees stand sentinel awaiting the summons of the spring.

*John Mitchell*

## PARADISE FOUND

The silver sands caress my toes,
The palm trees gently sway
The foaming tides adorn the shore
The sun beams down all day.

The seabirds swoop and soar, in flight,
Defying ocean breeze.
The breeze that sails a host of boats
And brings life to the trees.

Now, in those trees, a bed of life
Of multi-coloured wings.
A veritable artists scene
With all the joy it brings.

A paradise before my eyes
Fort me, a dream come true.
My dream of flights to foreign lands,
To start my life anew.

The scented flowers, like carpets lay
A rainbow on the ground.
No crock of gold, could e'er replace,
This Heaven I have found.

The garden here, of Eden stands
Its beauty bathes my mind.
Its sights and scents, like innocence,
Are all so hard to find.

Yet, here they are, in front of me
A haven for my soul.
A paradisic place to be
At last I've reached my goal.

*M J Plummer*

## EARLY MORNING MOMENTS IN MID DECEMBER

The will-o-the-wisp is drifting
From a clear as crystal pond,
And the mist of dawn is lifting
For the scarlet sun beyond
To rise above far distant hills
And frost encrusted leas,
Enough to see its splendour spills
In liquid light through storm-tossed trees.

The morning's silence, damp and still
Lies softly with rich scents of earth
Embalmed throughout its piercing chill,
With just the robin's tuneful mirth
Enough to tempt the frost-nipped ear
To listen to sweet notes, which ring,
With warmth and optimistic cheer
Which soothe them with the sounds of spring!

*Nicholas Winn*

## YESTERDAYS BEFORE TODAY

The canals I knew as a boy
Have long since gone.
I can recall them today
With great affection.

Many vivid memories remain
Of golden days
Spent at walks and play
Alongside its grassy ways.

Carefree, I followed winding paths,
Sometimes alone,
Exploring beyond the next bend
To a new zone.

I got to know its trails, reeds,
And bulrushes.
I watched moorhens and dragonflies,
Birds in its bushes.

We chased elusive minnows,
Even saw a few voles.
We were fascinated by frogs
And tiny tadpoles.

I recall too, when barges sailed
In earlier days,
Quietly transporting goods
By the waterways.

I can even remember
Barges pulled by horses,
Plodding along the banks,
Roped for the courses.

Alas! A different time.
A world gone forever.

Today on my visit
I followed the tracks
Of the canal I once knew.
Some bridges still there,
But now roads instead.
No sign of water,
Newcomers would not know.

I am glad there are still
Stretches of canals
Around the country,
Still barges to see,
Still nature to see,
But the canals I knew
Have long since gone.

***Terry Daley***

# ENGLISH COUNTRYSIDE

I see a meadow carpet flowered,
An ancient wood of oak and ash,
Birds in the air silhouette in sunshine,
Butterflies against the blue skies flash.

Kingfishers skim over babbling streams,
We can only wonder at such things,
No need to reason as to where or why,
Just enjoy this beauty as life goes by.

The earth has great things for us all to share,
With wonders around us everywhere,
The great whales in the oceans swim,
Where all fish and mammals live within.

To us this was given I know not why,
But grateful for these gifts am I,
We should preserve Earth's beauty as we all can,
And be proud we are the family of man.

But if events continue as in the past,
With war and destruction everywhere,
The Earth's Eco system will be destroyed,
And life on this world is bound to cease.

*Tony Pitt*

## NIGHT LIFE

Night falls silently
As I gaze into the widening, dark expanse
There's a spherical orb, in a starlit sky
I watch you circle, on a cloudless flight
Majestic and global, transferring your light
You scurry across a tabloid so dense
Picking out features, the lines by the fence
You chase the shadows, eclipsing the night
Encouraging creatures and demons to sight
A lone, weary traveller, scouring the streets
Looking for morsels, so tasty to eat.
And I see in the lines and the dips of the moon
A glimpse of your face, in the shadow and gloom
And I watch as gently you avoid your foe
In a moment, a cloud dips so darkness bestows
A calmness, a peace, an awe, a delight
So the fox no longer highlighted
Can frolic in a world free of plight
As the moon gently moves its path to refrain
The fox simply scurries to its den once again.

*Cate Campbell*

## NIGHTFALL OVER ULLSWATER

The evening sky
In its still-fading light
A prelude to
The darkness of night

The mist-softened hills
Sweep down to the shore
Fade into the waters
Where the edge is no more

A southern hill towers
Twinned there to make
A symmetrical image
Across the still lake

The last light of day
Falls over the deep
A late pair of ducks
Fly homeward to sleep

Ullswater waits
For the coming of night
The splendours of day
Have taken to flight

There in the quiet
Between night and day
There's majesty still
While the light fades away.

*Ray Ryan*

## LOOK AND SEE

I gaze at the rosy dawns
At the rainbow sunsets
At the blizzards on the glaciers
At the dark mountains
Grazing the sky,
A curtain shroud.
I crouch to touch the blue orchids, the gentians.
Inebriated with fresh air and beauty
I leap gleefully from rock to rock
Singing aloud
A friend smiles, 'The little deer is here!'

*A Matheson*

## DRAWN BY THE WAVES

As I gaze, wide-eyed,
At the increasingly receding waves,
They seem to drag me towards them,
Pulling me out, like a powerful magnet,
Sucking me slowly, and surely into . . .
And *under* the water,
Sucking me . . . into a watery grave;
Taking me into oblivion,
Away from my problems,
Away . . . into eternity.

My resistance is low.

*But . . . suddenly . . . I blink my eyes,*
*Snap! My mind breaks free!*
*Free from the breakers crashing on the shore!*

My freedom is not to be found
Under those waves,
It is to be found with You Lord,
In Your loving Presence
All around me.
You are in the waves
Speaking to me!

*J D Reeve*

## THE WAVES OF BURRY HOLMS

Rainbow on Rhossili arching over
the purple-green hills under a blue and grey sky.
But just like us it's transient and I watch it fade
into nothing to the tune of the wild, wintry wind.
Last time we made it to the rocks of Burry Holms
but now she turns back as the rain lashes again.
We tried to relight the flame but the past
is an empty chamber, the magic gone like the rainbow.
Now she only sees a desolate windswept beach,
she's by my side yet forever out of reach
under a dreary dome deep in winter
to the sound of a lone gull's lament.

I walk on, the beauty here still consumes me,
the sun shining through on the horizon like search lights
and the foam chasing each other like lambs at play
to the chorus of raging wind and roaring sea.
Burry Holms is now obscured by slashing rain
as I watch the vague reflections on the wet sand
and listen to the fizz of the rhythmic waves
as they reach their journey's end.

A flock of birds fly off from the shore
and a pony and sheep graze on the cliffs
as I trudge on, the vast lonely beach
making distances deceptive. My footprints
are the only ones in the sand today.
The waves of Burry Holms pound mightily
trying to reach the bleak cliff-top
but my gaze returns from the cold, grey ocean
to see a distant figure on the uncaring sand,
the past is an empty chamber, a different land.

*Guy Fletcher*

## WHAT A WONDERFUL WORLD!

When you see the silent sea horses,
Weenie wonders of the deep,
Or the gently waving fronds of coral
On a barrier reef:
When you ponder on the miracle
Of a baby seal asleep:
Or see the myriad colours
Of a falling Autumn leaf:
Can you doubt there is a purpose
In this magic world of ours
As you think about the perfume
And the delicacy of flowers?

When you watch a spinning spider
Weave its web of filmy lace:
Or peer in ponderous moments
At a baby's smiling face.
When you see the awesome anger
Of the turbulent raging sea:
Or remember swaying barley
Upon the Summer lea.
Can you fathom out the mystery
Of a swirling flock of birds
Climbing, soaring, diving -
Just a beauty beyond words:

As you watch a strutting seagull
As it 'Lords' upon the sands
In the fading twilight
Skies streaked with silvery bands.
As you listen to the silence
Of a frosty starlit night
Or watch the new dawn breaking
In bursts of golden light

Then you know there is a purpose
In everything unfurled
In this, our beauteous planet
Our great wide Wonderful World!

*Mollie D Earl*

## WATERWORLD

Acid rain falls to earth
destroying the green life
of our world . . .
the foul rainfall is engendered
by big fat cat profits
for the favoured few.

Deadly clouds
of greenhouse gas
are spewed from factories
and over crowded roads
creating dramatic climate change
as Mother Earth heats up.

Global warming increases
and the ice fields start to thaw
making sea levels rise
and starting to drown
low lying lands
and threatening to overwhelm
the higher dry lands.

The oceans gather strength
striving to make the earth
a spinning globe of water
with no trace of humankind
and free of man's toxic waste.

In the near future
it will be waterworld
spinning its cosmic path
around the solar system
with no trace of land
or beast or man . . .

*Stephen Gyles*

# THE FLIGHT

The plane it droned as onward it did speed,
The cabin door locked tight and sealed by bar
Shut out the old world, letting it recede,
As on it flew towards new lands afar.
The couple sat and wondered whether they
Had done the right thing, emigrating thus,
To leave their home and roots so far away,
Embark with all they owned on this airbus.
The life they faced, how would it quite compare
With what they'd left behind? And what if they
Disliked the people, weather, job or where
They'd live, most like, forever and a day?
He smiled at her. 'The past is past,' he said,
'When that door opens, it's our watershed.'

***Christopher Head***

## FRIEND AND ENEMY

Like a great eternal dance is the rhythm of the sea.
Expressing tranquil passion, or violent ecstasy.
A song comes softly sighing through its many harmonies,
And orchestras are playing in the music of the sea.

Its glory all is borrowed from the beauty of the sky.
In changing shades of green, grey, blue with white foam
                                                    drifting by.
Reflected on its surface gold sunlight's sparkling fires,
A moonlight sheds a path of light across its dark desires.

In mystery, serenity, ferocity and peace.
In playfulness and menace, tides and currents never cease.
Don't trust your mind; just trust your heart to understand the sea.
It speaks to the emotions, is both friend and enemy.

*Irene Seager*

# CATCH A FALLING STAR

As the sun sets over the world
No matter where you are
Try to find the time
To take a look at the stars.

These small like diamonds
Glittering in the sky
Are one of the most amazing sights
To be seen by the naked eye.

So many miles away
It is hard to comprehend
That if they ever disappeared
Would the world come to an end.

For these natural beauties
Make the world seem so special
Just hope that when you are watching
That one should chance to fall.

If it does then I am sure
All your dreams will come true
And never will you ever forget
The stars are there for you.

*Ian Fowler*

## DOWN TO THE WOODS

We've been this way many times before
Off the beaten track not knowing what's in store.
Walking as far as we can go.
There's always something new on show.
All we envisage far and near,
Is to see that herd of deer.
The path that we made to lead you through.
Will one day be a floor of bells so blue.
On a branch up above comes a blackbird's song,
That encourages and coaxes us along.
Perhaps in a far distant day,
Our grandchildren will walk this woodland way.
Rotting bark from trees of bygone days,
Let's in the sunshine's warm rays.
Peace and tranquillity of no other kind,
We love to sit and enjoy peace of mind.
Nothing but birds and the odd butterfly,
We look up at the beauty of the sky.
There's a stream that trickles a small flow,
Then finds it has nowhere to go.
A raised embankment where ivy grows along the ground,
It's creeped up trees without making a sound.
What a lovely sight a chirping bird in her nest,
We enjoy the beauty of it while we take a rest.
An old tree with rotting branches, what a loss,
This broken down tree is now covered in moss.
In its day it would have stood proud,
Missed by folk who walk the right way round
We long for days when we can go and just sit,
And look in wonder, how nature's done her bit.

*Jenny Noble*

# WAVE OF EMOTION

Gentle rustle
Powerful surge
Soft white bubbles
Tempting urge.

Stand in awe
Listen and stare
Hear the strength
Breathe the air.

Plunge deep to fulfil
Pure and clear
Deadly beauty
A price so dear.

Awash with feeling
In sweep and curl
Swathed in panic
Sucking swirl.

It may be beauteous
Constant motion
But never seek
To defy the ocean.

For she has been
For many years
And she'll live on
Amid salty tears.

*Tanya Fowles*

## WORLD

All the places, all the people, all the beauty,
inspire me to write, I consider it my duty.
To share with others, the feelings evoked,
oak-like smell of bacon, freshly smoked.
Swathes of spring flowers, swaying,
position of a mantis, when praying.

Loving, tender, seductive women,
grace of dolphins, simply swimming.
Moon, stars, hidden galaxies above,
all the intricacies, of human love.
Development of a conceived baby foetus,
fighting for life, preparing to meet us.

It's all inspiration, all fascination,
all open, to individual interpretation.
Love it or loathe it, it's here to stay,
I'm going to make the most of it,
'Til my dying day.

*Danny Coleman*

## CAME THE DAWN

I seize the moment
And capture a dream
And witness the beauty when the morning does yawn
The sun kept a promise awoke from its sleep
Light kissed the horizon and thus came the dawn

I saw a conception an angelic world
Creeping from the darkness to saturate my eyes
Like a newborn moment aspiring to life
This is my treasure my dream and my prize

I heard a chorus
Introducing the day
A fine feathered choir betrothed to one voice
Hymns written by nature to entice the mood
Of an exalted happiness asked to rejoice

I feel a presence its beauty and love
As I do trespass where the morning is crowned
I probe the experience of a privileged few
And the pleasure of belonging in this ritual surround

I breathe the aroma
The prayer of a flower
A spiritual love that is passed to another
A pure touch of creation brushed by sublime
Whose natural innocence explodes into colour

I drink the memory of this brief masterpiece
A morning coronation that my presence adorns
A taste of satisfaction a dream blessed by life
The sun kept a promise and thus came the dawn

*David Bridgewater*

## OUR WORLD

I look at the beauty displayed
        all around me,
The flowers with their faces turned
        up to the sun,
The hills and the mountains, the
        green river valleys,
The seas, and the shores where
        children have fun.

I listen to music from nature's own
        orchestra,
The birds singing sweetly, the hum of
        the bees,
The ripple of streams flowing through
        grassy meadows,
Where crickets chirrup loudly beneath
        rustling trees.

The scents of the summer drift into
        my nostrils,
The flowery perfume and the freshly
        cut grass
I stroll through an orchard inhaling
        the sweet smell
Of the fruit, and savour the delights
        as I pass.

I reach out and touch the bark of
        a tree,
And velvety rose petals caress my
        hand.
I drink the cool water that wells
        from a spring,
And eat of the harvest, hard-worked
        from the land.

For this the work of
        our loving Creator.
Who gave such beauty for us to
        behold,
And each of our senses with which
        to enjoy it,
Our God's in His heaven, all's right,
        with the world.

*Audrey Coe*

## NEVER THE SAME

Never two hours the same, never two days,
　　Never two winters, never two waking springs,
Never two bluebells which delight our gaze,
　　Never two raptures as a blackbird sings.

Never the same regrets as summer ends,
　　Not the same leaf which from the oak tree flies,
Never the same, the joy of greeting friends,
　　Nor the same sorrow when a loved one dies.

Never the same, a single daisy flower,
　　Never the same, the taste of crusty bread,
Never repeated, our most joyful hour,
　　Never unchanged, the loving words we said.

Yet still the same, the things which touch our hearts
　　The joys and sorrows, common to our kind;
Beyond our comprehension, myriad parts
　　Which speak forever of a guiding Mind.

No drop of water, no, nor grain of sand,
　　No sunrise shouting its integrity,
But gives the message, written by His Hand,
　　The same yet ever new, eternally.

*Kathleen M Hatton*

## GREEN SAVIOUR

A sacred thought rests upon the grass so green.
It is so beautiful and greener than green.
Grass stands like a divine forest so tall,
And yet, to mammalian life, it is so small.

It holds a silky sensation so soft and well bred.
In its grassy flanks many insects make their bed.
Grass ascending and completely obscuring an old boot.
Grass dances a sensual dance when the wind journeys
                            through its root.

Grass is a vast sea which lays upon a land lost.
Sometimes its parched by the sun or bitten by frost.
Grass sings its own secret, silent tune,
And sleeps calmly beneath a shimmering silver moon.

*Peter Steele*

## THE EPITOME OF CREATION

He gave me ten fingers to work and toil
Making beauty from things and soil,
He gave me eyes his world to view
Each day brings what's fresh and new,
He gave me two ears to listen well,
Something to learn, something to tell,
He gave me a tongue to praise and bless,
Words that soothe like a caress,
He gave me a heart that beats so well,
A cosmic clockwork, a rhythmic spell,
He gave us a skin so smooth to feel
This changing world, a dream so real,
He gave me feet to bear the news
And two thick soles to act as shoes,
He gave me a mate to share my love,
It links the earth to heaven above,
A mind to reason, guide the whole,
Each organ faithful to its role,
He gave me a soul to feed and grow
His wondrous works to gaze and know,
Pain and pleasure to show the way,
Thank Him for his gifts today.

*Emmanuel Petrakis*

## CALFE HEY TRAIL

I've never done it the golden oldies route before
pausing to look at the foundations in the earth
life, living, and community before the dam
not paused before to really enter this living past into my centre
to literally dwell here like those of old
no, I've swung up the path through the trees
to hill top, open moors and adventure;
only today, it was either the golden oldies route
or it was not doing it at all; exhausted.

Yet, to my surprise, having hidden this till now,
it really was even lovelier from ground level,
the incarnation really clicked
the sheep tracks and lost ways were mine
and so was my way with the shepherd.

*Robert D Shooter*

## LITTLE ONE

Little one,
I hold you in my arms
And feel your form,
Softness wrapped in silkiness
Calm after storm.
I smell the sweetness of your skin
So smooth and pure
And kiss the velvet of your face
Feeling you stir

Little one,
So heavy, yet so light and small
Though silent lying in my arms
I heard you call
For you my heart
Will ever bear a burden
Full of love,
You captured me with one
Sweet tiny breath
My little dove.

*Christine Dennison*

# LEAVES

As they sleep swaying in
the wind on a tall long branch

Time pasts by time to wake up,
breaking though like a butterfly
to the warmth of the sun shining
down, and the current of the wind
and rain, they live and breath as nature allows.

***Olive Irwin***

## THE SAVAGE SEA

She seemed so calm and still
Basking beneath the summer skies
Gently stroking the life she hides below
Until rousing from her tranquil sleep
A hunger begins to stir within
A hunger that slowly begins to swell within her depths
Gathering in size, rising through the smooth surface
Erupting into an anger that no man will tame
With the anger of a raging beast
She begins the forward surge
To her destiny
Her once peaceful rolling waves have now become
Ferocious thundering rolls of death, plunging onward
Long watery arms claw their way onto wind lashed
Sodden beaches searching for an offering
Retreating only to throw themselves closer to the shore
Over and over again, crashing waves, determined
To destroy everything in their path, rise to terrifying heights
Then with horrendous roars of satisfaction
Collapse in an orgy of destruction
Leaving behind her a void, a silence
Her sacrifice claimed, she could now return
To her dark depths far beneath
Restoring her still waters
If this was once a heaven
She surely brought with her a hell.

*Wendy Smith*

## SUMMER'S DAWN

The call of the wood pigeon,
     breaks the silence,
Of an early summer's day morn,
Flowers, raise their heads from stalk pillows,
To answer the sunlight's early morning call.

A haze, crosses the horizon,
As the mid day heat, begins beating down,
Mirages form - to confuse the vision,
Eyesight - lost in familiar surrounds.

The earth's soil surrenders,
To form a crust of hardened brown,
As the previous night's rainfalls attempts
     to remain as moisture,
No longer can be found.

Summer, resplendent in all its glory,
Winter's effots, banished to hiding
     in pockets of shade,
As the sun's rays, mirrored in the
     ripples of the river's flowing waters,
Sparkle, as they dance on victory parade.

*Bakewell Burt*

## GOD'S WONDERFUL FREE GIFTS

The best things in life are those that are free.
There for the taking, for you, and for me.
Nature's beauties which surround us each day,
Like those wonderful sunsets with dying ray.
Bright spring flowers after dull winter days
Song birds on tree blossom, our spirits to raise
Watching the endless tide from cliff top high,
Waves crashing on rocks below as they draw nigh.
Solitude in woodland, with bluebell and wild flower.
Away from worldly cares, to spend a quiet hour
Sailing ships silhouetted against fading light,
As darkness falls, drifting way into night,
Star-studded sky, harvest moon so bright,
Putting to shame the old street light,
The perfect rainbow after heavy shower,
Symbol to us of God's mighty power,
Autumn's glorious tints of russet and red.
A colourful leafed carpet on which to tread
Breathtaking scenery of mountain and stream,
Cascading waterfall, like an exquisite dream.
Hoar frosted landscape, all glistening white.
Nature's canvas displaying a spectacular sight.
Scenes of incredible beauty when covered in snow,
Making our hearts and finger's glow.
How fortunate we are these beauties to possess,
To console and comfort us, in times of stress.

*E Kathleen Jones*

# EVENSONG

Sunset, crimson slashed clouds
Fading into pale grey twilight
Enfolded in evening mists.

Beyond shadowed hills
The last sounds of evening
Sheep bells echo. Dogs bark.
A late truck thunders past.

Edging roads and byways
A tracery of lights
Brighten in sudden darkness.

Behind cloud streaks
Early stars glimmer.
Moon glow,
Patches of silver, touch hills.

Sudden breezes rustle leaves.
Dark shadows dance on terrace tiles.
Wind bells chime. Little owl shrieks.

Now all is silent, all asleep.
Hill and valley washed in silver light.
Moonbeams caught among tree branches
Shine in through my window.

*A J Roberts*

## EVENING FOX-TROT

I saw him by the Adur
with a rabbit in his jaws,
his red tail proud and bushy
as he loped without a pause.

His eyes were two green almonds
his head erect with pride,
as he carried home his victim
by the misty riverside.

Through rushes by the river
bank, he made a graceful leap,
his lifeless bundle swaying
as he neared a flock of sheep.

He didn't seem to worry
when he saw me by the stile,
although he kept his distance -
and I swear I saw him smile.

And then he seemed to vanish
in the long grass - hid from men;
was a hungry vixen waiting
with her fox cubs in the den?

*Jonathan Bryant*

## MY EDEN

I love to walk the mountain paths
  far from the urban scene
Enjoying the works of nature
  in a location that's serene
To see the different wild flowers
  and the animals running free
Is magic to my prying eyes
  and is food and drink to me
To see the foaming cataracts
  from the flowing mountain rills
Creates a magnitude of beauty
  that is a sight to thrill
To see the eagle up aloft
  in its domain up on high
One can see how it is dubbed
  the king of all the sky
The deer grazing on the mountain slopes
  are alert to all around
Ready to make a dash for it
  if there is an alien sound
This landscape is my Eden
  my love for this won't fade
I only hope with those modern trends
  no changes will be made.

*Lachlan Taylor*

## PICTURES OF YESTERYEAR

As I sit back with eyelids closed,
of memories there are magical loads.
Pictures come rushing back,
of beauties past which I did think I did lack.

Those heavenly days which were full of bliss,
or perhaps you recall that first heartfelt kiss.
Those glorious landscape views,
which to you was always the best of news.

The lovely sunsets of red and gold,
which were always there in days of old.
As you travelled a lot when you were young,
your days always appeared so full of fun.

Never give in - keep your happiness fresh,
you think you are embroiled in a mesh?
But when you remember days so very dear,
your path will appear so very clear.

*Betty Green*

## A FLOOD-PLAIN PICTURE

There goes a tree trunk
hurtling down a stream
the odd piece of debris
remnants of somebody's dream
there goes a tyre
there goes the wheel of a pram
a recipe for disaster
a man-made scrap metal dam
there goes a shoe
a gate, once used for kissing
also, a motor car
a means of travel, gone missing
a boat goes down the street
a fire engine becomes stranded
batten down the hatches
the apocalypse has landed
no need to mow the lawn
flood water hides the lawn
even the diversions
are quite difficult to pass.

*Trevor Vincent*

## My Garden Birds

Little robin with your breast bright red
hopping nearer hoping to be fed
finding a crumb then flying away
you remind me of Christmas day

Grey sparrows picking around the logs
keeping a watchful eye for our dogs
my pure white doves strutting everywhere
cooing and dancing without a care

The magpies are smart in black and white
(hopping along . . . a comical sight)
swallows flying, low insects to find
blue tits perching on my washing line

Goldfinches which like to pick the seeds
(here's an excuse not to root out the weeds)
the thrush on the stone taps out the snails
and watchful kestrel overhead sails

Skylarks that sing all the summer days
climbing so high in the misty haze
blackbirds, starlings and tiny wee wren
are all close when my garden I tend.

*Valerie Ovais*

## THE WILDERNESS

Beauty, colour all around,
Birds singing in the trees,
Peace, tranquillity abound,
Hot sun, refreshing breeze.

Mountain's reach toward the sky
With undulating peaks,
Always changing by and by,
While God His vigil keeps.

Water lapping on the beach,
Majestic rocks stand out,
This is all within our reach,
Thanks to our God we shout.

Every breath we take each day
It is a God sent gift,
Let us to you homage pay,
Our souls to you we lift.

Knowing you are always there,
Guiding us to the light,
May we always love and care
Each morning, noon and night.

***Suzanne Joy Golding***

# WATER LIFE

I sailed the lakes around my native Bala,
went to sea on waters of a different colour.
The smell of the sea is so different from the land,
and yet both have been made by God's own hand.

One day I'll wander the seas no more;
to walk the land that I knew before.
Much has changed since I went to sea,
but the biggest change has been in me.

*J R Waterman*

## DANCING WITH THE WIND

Grey sky, just a light breeze,
Open country, there is a hill . . . there,
All covered with heather, still flowering.
I could walk by.

Charmed by the colour . . . of the heather,
Tempted by the narrow path, I walk up.
Just the natural sounds.
I reach the top. Suddenly

I am looking down at swallows,
Swallows are flying . . . all around me,
So close at times, we can almost touch.
Swallows just doing . . . what they do.

Above the heather tiny flies can be seen,
Dancing . . . dancing with the wind.

*Claire-Lyse Sylvester*

## CYPRUS SUN

Sunny days
In a golden haze
Deep blue seas
A light warm breeze
Warm white stones
With grey-pink tones
Soft lapping sea
We sat on a rock, just you and me
Aphrodite, Goddess of ages past
Weaved a spell
And under we fell
We hoped this moment would
Forever be
And so we made love
You and me
From that day my heart was won
Under the spell of the Cyprus sun.

*Judith Bradley*

## RHOSSILI BAY

Over springy soft grass
a pathway I tread,
one step forward into another world.

Solitude kindles my soul,
The awesome majesty of an ocean blue,
enveloped by fluffy drifting clouds.
Sea thrifts carpet rugged grey cliffs,
screeching gulls pierce my ears.
Alone with my thoughts, I embrace
the beauty of nature around me.

Salt sea-air invigorates my lungs,
a yearning to explore
the mystical world beyond.

Pace by pace, a steep ridge I climb,
far below, echoes of whispering waves.
On the distant horizon, the sun
weaves a tapestry of exotic gold.
Spellbound, I look and look again,
before me, a massive black rock
carved as an evil monster,
anchored in the ocean depths.

Little time to reflect, nature is calling,
journey's end is almost in sight.
Listen, a chorus of oystercatchers
busily scrounging amidst craggy rocks.
Above me the heavens, below the sea,
waves gently lapping my feet,
a solitary figure in a world of my own.

*Diana Frewin*

## BEAUTY UNSEEN

The beauty of our countryside, is passed unseen
Forests, and meadows, lush and green
Flora, and fauna, that delight the eye
The miracle, that is life, passes swiftly by

Trains and automobiles, moving faster and faster
Often ending in a complete disaster
No time to look at nature's gift
Without a care, on an ocean adrift

Just pause and stop for a while
Walk the footpath, climb over the stile
A world of beauty, teeming with life
Away from all the pressure, and strife.

Bring a stop to the hustle and bustle
Out of your seat, and move a muscle
Take a deep breath, of country air
Before driving off, adding pollution to the layer.

*T W Evans*

## LATE AUTUMN

Sycamore leaves - yellow stars,
illumine the river bank.
Grey-green waters
tumble over lichened stones.
Phosphorus spray-incandescent jewels
kiss my face.

Cackling crows crack the silence
and remind the weather glass
that winter, in his
dark and sombre robe
will soon be here.

On Elm, few leaves dare to remain,
like baubles on a Christmas tree,
tinsel bright, to and froing,
outwitting the talons of wind and rain.

Cat and dogs fly
with this seasonal friend.
Winter, friend of autumn
waits in her tempestuous skirts
ready to pounce again.

**Alison Cameron**

## A WINTER'S TALE

Softly fell the gentle snow, penetrating Jack Frost
Bitterly biting easterly winds whining like crying souls lost

Battering blizzards, deep snowdrifts, frozen lake and river
Hedgerows, trees bedecked, sparkling cobwebs shimmer

Frozen pipes, slippery paths, black iced roads
Cars abandoned, lorries stranded with heavy loads

Frozen points delaying InterCity trains
Busy hospitals mending broken bones and easing pains

Still magical quietness of white wonderland
Broken by delighted children's whoops
Many coloured bobbled woolly hats
Bobbing down white slippery slopes

Snow boarding, sledging, tobogganing
Screams of delight, children's happiness overflowing.

*K G Johnson*

## DOWN STREAM

A favourite place of mine;
That comes to mind
Is where the stream, twists and winds.
Below the tall trees,
The stream over seen by, million leisurely leaves,
Of lofty hornbeams.
Around the zig-zag bends of the roaring stream.
That washed away the clay flanking banking.
The slashes of crumbling, tumbling banks.
Exposing a tangle, cruel knotted roots.
Of wired looking sculpture shapes.
Look at then, as long as it takes.
See whatever sculpture the imagination makes.
See where the banks have caved away,
An oak fallen, over the bubbling swift water way.
Forming a creaking swaying natural bridge.
Supervised by dads, shouting kids,
Shouting with joy,
As they run down the slopes.
Commando style, across the stream swing on ropes.
One kid's cry of burnt hands on the rope.
Without doubt.
A place to run and shout.
Unconcerned on small gravel island grids.
Wagtails feeding on water shrimps, mid-stream.
Crows swoop down too search.
For red blood worms.
Under the pebbles by the stream.
One can only look and learn.

*B G Clarke*

## MY LOVELY WORLD

I stood upon a lonely hill
And felt the breeze upon my face.
The sky larks thrilled me with their song
In this delightful place
The air was filled with butterflies
And perfume from wildflowers,
Pink orchids, cowslips and a rose
I wished the day would never close
On these enchanted hours.

A deer appeared upon the hill,
While rabbits cropped the grass,
And all the ladybirds and bees
Hoped the day would never pass ,
The cuckoo whispered to the trees
That summer must be here to stay
To make this such a perfect day.

*Beryl Williams*

## MORNING IN NERJA

They nestle closely to the sun-drenched hills
And shimmer in an aureole of light.
The white-washed houses seem to float on air,
Like magic castles beautiful and bright.

Majestic mountains lift their craggy heads,
Like sculptured Titans guarding their domain.
Their lofty ramparts, wreathed in shifting clouds,
Echo the whisper of the wind's refrain.

The varied tinctures of the timeless sea
Will change chameleon-like from blue to green,
From sapphire to emerald to jade,
Its glassy surface sparkling and serene.

Meanwhile the waking town is full of sound,
Resounding to the old familiar beat
Of donkeys' hooves which tap a tympany
With rhythmic cloppings on the cobbled street.

Life celebrates its joy with gorgeous hues -
The flowers, the fruits, the glowing orange trees,
And multi-coloured, gauzy butterflies
Which spread their wings to hover on the breeze.

Now feathered clouds marble the Wedgwood sky,
And fading moon discreetly hides his face.
The morning mists drift down to touch the sea
And there, like phantoms, vanish without trace.

*Celia G Thomas*

## THE MILLENNIUM FLOOD

I'm sure, it is clear,
We'll remember *this* year:
The gathering cloud
Over fields freshly ploughed,
Then, the deluge came
And, much more of the same.
In Africa, America, Asia,
In Britain, Europe and Australia
Fields turned to lakes,
Roads became rivers.
People clung to trees and roofs
Waiting in hope of rescue.
Crops were washed away
In less than a day.
People's homes were destroyed
Aid was slowly deployed.
But, then came more rain
And again and again.
We were short of wetlands,
But not anymore.

*Catherine Blackett*

## ABOUNDING BEAUTY

Golden glow of the morning sun
Blue of the ocean waves
Whiteness of snow
Weaving through the pine forest
Leaving long winding furrows ploughman unseen
Beauty of rainbow reflecting on raindrops
Beauty of stars in a wintry sky
Beauty all around there's abounding beauty
Beautiful music in a new born baby's cry
Beauty of sunset behind snow-capped mountain
Sheep seeking shelter from flurries of snow
Rivers of crystal murmuring and turning
Hurrying homeward to their vast ocean home
Looking around through transcending beauty
Painted designed by our Father above
Most of all God's love surrounds us
He sent His own son to die on the cross
All who believes a pardon receives
Then a mansion above to dwell in God's love throughout Eternity

*Frances Gibson*

## PERFECTLY SQUARE WORLD

Around me, this world. My world. A square
Framed and roofed by five surrounding squares.
Sensitively sense-based is my square world.

In its warm and feather-soft, fertile ground,
I plant thought-seeds that spout and grow,
Of types, tastes and tunes that make me glow

Which live out dreams from nine till five, then
Late at nights and certain unsleepful dawns
From this satin-lined seat one sees in my square.

My square is flush with ungrowling shelves,
Cuddling books, piling files, screens, pens,
Papers, trophies, snaps and puzzles-in-paint.

Time goes to sleep in my cosy square, when
Hunger dies, thirst dries up, and thwarting
Pains never breathe. Gloom, seldom blooms.

My square's my heaven, my carefree world
Of inspiring souls in an incense-filled bliss
Where thoughts alone live and mind reigns.

My square. My world. My square world.

*Kopan Mahadeva*

## EPITAPH TO THE CREW OF A LANCASTER

Were you not afraid,
To dare the fates.
To laugh at danger.
Think not of heaven's gates,
But listen to the engines roar
Of that which took you
From our shore.

In reckless youth
Think not to die,
But hungry for adventure,
Took up the challenge
Of the battle
In the sky.

In silence now
No Merlins sound.
Stark the white memorials stand.
To those who shared
As comrades fear,
But never blanched,
From duty bound.

Lie side by side.
One common bond.
In foreign soil, each to the other.
Each spirit, free, for freedom given.
Now lie at peace, each as his brother.
To those who once together flew.
Undivided, still, in death, one crew.

*Gwyneth Pritchard*

## A PEA

'Twas only just a little pea which fell from out the pod
And bending down to pick it up, my thoughts then turned to God
In wondering who had drawn the plans, to programme this small seed
Designed to grow from fertile soil and form a plant . . . indeed,
To flower: spring high: form many pods, to nurse the young within,
Where season's growth completes God's will, then peas to fall, ad fin.

'Twas only just a little thought when bending down so low
That time was taken thinking why these green peas had to grow.
To fall to earth by gravity in sizes great and small
By wind and tempest, nature's way, or even nature's call.
But fall they will to rise again, as seasons come and go,
To tax the back, then mind again, yet, life is ever so.

Up and down no matter what, or where we sweat and toil.
We all grow old with aching bones, to get buried 'neath the soil.
To rise again, live life anew, no matter where or when.
The problem is, that no one knows,
$\qquad\qquad\qquad$ When we'll be back again.

*D Turberfield*

# SUBMISSIONS INVITED
## *SOMETHING FOR EVERYONE*

**POETRY NOW 2001** - Any subject,
any style, any time.

**WOMENSWORDS 2001** - Strictly women,
have your say the female way!

**STRONGWORDS 2001** - Warning!
Age restriction, must be between 16-24,
opinionated and have strong views.
(Not for the faint-hearted)

All poems no longer than 30 lines.
Always welcome! No fee!
Cash Prizes to be won!

Mark your envelope (eg *Poetry Now) 2001*
Send to:
Forward Press Ltd
Remus House, Coltsfoot Drive,
Peterborough, PE2 9JX

## OVER £10,000 POETRY PRIZES
## TO BE WON!

Judging will take place in October 2001